WHEN SATURN RETURNS

WHEN SATURN RETURNS

Surviving Your Astrological Coming-of-Age

David Odyssey

Illustrations by Satwika Kresna

CHRONICLE BOOKS
SAN FRANCISCO

Copyright © 2025 by David Goldberg.

All rights reserved. No part of this book may be reproduced in any form without written permission from the publisher.

Library of Congress Cataloging-in-Publication Data

Names: Odyssey, David, author. | Kresna, Satwika, illustrator.
Title: When Saturn Returns : surviving your astrological coming-of-age / David Odyssey ; illustrations by Satwika Kresna.
Description: San Francisco : Chronicle Books, [2025]
Identifiers: LCCN 2024037660 | ISBN 9781797231617 (hardcover)
Subjects: LCSH: Saturn (Planet)--Miscellanea. | Astrology. | Self-actualization (Psychology)
Classification: LCC BF1724.2.S3 O294 2025 | DDC 133.5/37--dc23/eng/20241015
LC record available at https://lccn.loc.gov/2024037660

Manufactured in China.

Design by Maggie Edelman.

Illustrations by Satwika Kresna.

10 9 8 7 6 5 4 3 2 1

Chronicle books and gifts are available at special quantity discounts to corporations, professional associations, literacy programs, and other organizations. For details and discount information, please contact our premiums department at corporategifts@chroniclebooks.com or at 1-800-759-0190.

Chronicle Books LLC
680 Second Street
San Francisco, California 94107
www.chroniclebooks.com

For my mother, father, and stepmother

CONTENTS

INTRODUCTION
When Saturn Returns 9

HOW TO USE THIS BOOK 11

Part One: SATURN
Meet Your Terminator 17
Interpreting Saturn 21
Tracking Saturn 25
The Three Saturn Returns in Your Life 29

Part Two: WHEN SATURN RETURNS TO THE SIGNS
The Signs 35
Aries 40
Taurus 48
Gemini 56
Cancer 64
Leo 72
Virgo 80
Libra 88
Scorpio 96
Sagittarius 104
Capricorn 112
Aquarius 120
Pisces 128

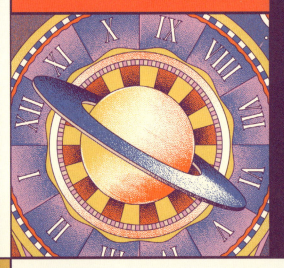

Part Three:
WHEN SATURN RETURNS TO THE HOUSES

The Houses 139
First House 142
Second House 148
Third House 154
Fourth House 160
Fifth House 166
Sixth House 172
Seventh House 178
Eighth House 184
Ninth House 190
Tenth House 196
Eleventh House 202
Twelfth House 208

Part Four:
WHEN SATURN HITS THE PLANETS

Saturn and the Personal Planets 217

Saturn and the Generational Planets 227

Conclusion:
SATURN INCARNATE 232

Glossary 234
Acknowledgments 238
About the Author 240

INTRODUCTION

When Saturn Returns

In the midst of all this insanity, a couple of things are starting to make sense.
—*Buffy the Vampire Slayer*

There seems to be a collective consensus among those of us who have surpassed age thirty-three: Certain years bring the heat. Age fourteen launches the rebellion, twenty-one the discovery. Twenty-eight to thirty is the revolution. Things fall apart, things come together. Your career changes, you end your first major relationship, you realize the hangovers aren't worth the party, you move to a new country. You become less blurry.

Naturally, astrology has an answer for every one of life's crossroads, likely down to the minute. There are ten planets and endless asteroids coursing through our solar system, all informing some archetypal meaning down here on terra firma. In witnessing the orbit of the planets, we understand time not as a linear progression but an endless cycle, its closings immediately yielding new beginnings.

But some cycles are more dramatic than others. The most infamous awakening of all comes when the planet Saturn completes its three-decade revolution around the zodiac, returning to its starting position at the moment when you were born. Saturn is the planet of form and efficiency. It knows your function and how you're (probably) failing to fulfill it. Your first Saturn Return is something of a cosmic check-in, a review of how you've lost your way over these past thirty years and what must be done to realign with your destined service.

Live long enough, and you'll be fortunate to experience three Saturn Returns in your lifetime, two more rotations to challenge everything you think you know: one in your late fifties and one in your eighties. These transits are meant to strip away that which no longer serves you, and deliver you anew to your purpose on this mortal coil.

Despite these pivotal returns, Saturn is always moving through the heavens, and its drive toward redefinition is ever affecting you and the larger culture around you. Even if you're not in your Saturn Return era, Saturn is hard at work in some aspect of your life. This book tracks Saturn's every configuration. It is meant to be flipped through over and over and accessed afresh so that you may come to understand the call going out to you with every change of season, and the assignment of every age. It is my intention to light your way, to offer perspective, and to halt the reflex for self-victimization and despair. You already have everything you need to face what Saturn brings. I'm just giving you some context.

The practice of astrology is to interpret meaning based on the dance of the planets through the sky. Based on any given planet's location when you were born, we can gain endless insight about your characteristics or heart's desires. Moreover, if we consider where the planets are right now, we can contemplate the current challenges and opportunities laid out before you. As a working astrologer, I have had the privilege to counsel hundreds of clients through their Saturn Return sagas. But beyond what any professional experience could teach me, I speak to you as an on-going survivor of Saturn's trials. I have experienced my fair share of humiliation and humility, loss and rebirth—at least enough to offer my empathy for whatever Saturn throws your way. As with all my clients, I am here to voyage *with* you, to learn as we go, and not to pretend that I can teach you any lessons. That's Saturn's job.

HOW TO USE THIS BOOK

If Saturn is the planet of adulthood, then this book is your guide to growing up. And while you may have (wisely) purchased this book in preparation for your impending Saturn Return, no one will ever be "grown-up" enough to break loose from Saturn's grip, so this book is designed to be a continuous resource throughout your life. Saturn will always be returning *somewhere*.

With this book in hand, you will better understand Saturn's ever-shifting influence—from a cultural and societal level all the way down to the individual. Each of us is a part of a larger ecosystem, and Saturn will help you grow in harmony with the world around you. Right now, as you read this very sentence, Saturn is impacting you in ways that you haven't yet begun to reckon with, and will continue to do so through every stage of your life to come.

The introductory chapters reveal Saturn's nature and the characteristics that make it a cosmic force destined to propel our evolution, both collectively and individually. Here, we lay the foundation and time frame through which we perceive the planet. With a grip on what Saturn is, we can find meaning in its interactions with astrology's key players: the signs, houses, and other planets.

Following Saturn's orbit, we start with the zodiac. The twelve signs are fixed points in the heavens, which all the planets pass through on their individual cycles. Some planets, like Venus and Mercury, spend only weeks in each sign, while Saturn's residencies last about three years. The combination of Saturn's extended duration and the planet's unique characteristics when it crosses a sign will impact our culture at large and spell out the dominant moral discourse and social changes of the moment. The signs chapters explore the last 100+ years of human history through Saturn transits, offering insight into the generational, collective, and individual lessons the planet has in store. You will learn to follow Saturn's crossing through all the signs, recognizing the challenges and triumphs that await you in every phase of life. We will use history to not only interpret what is going on in the world today but also anticipate the shape of things to come.

You can determine Saturn's location—when you were born, now, and in years to come—by checking the dates listed in each sign chapter. For instance, if you were born in March 2001, you'd find your birthday in the Saturn-in-Taurus chapter. In the same list of dates, you'd see that Saturn next returns to Taurus in 2028. This will be the arena of your Saturn Return. Your sun sign and Saturn sign may be different. On the blessed day when Cher was born, the sun was in Taurus and Saturn was in Cancer. So Cher would identify as a Taurus, but she would want to read about her upcoming third Saturn Return in this book's Cancer chapter.

The signs are just the beginning. To understand Saturn's specific assignment for you, we will move on to the houses that represent different areas of your life. Everyone has a birth chart, a personal map of the stars at the moment they were born, which can be calculated for free online. With your chart in hand, you can see where Saturn is currently at work in your life, what unique blind spots it seeks to address, and the calling made for only you to answer.

Finally, we'll consider Saturn's interactions with the other planets of your chart, each representing a different facet of your character. Saturn's collisions with these archetypes lead to periods of intense challenge and earned renewal. We lay out the qualities of each planet and imagine how their clashes with Saturn affect you intimately.

Whether you're graduating college or readying for retirement, you're definitely going through *something*. While you may or may not be in your Saturn Return, the fundamental assignments of every chapter still apply. Say you're twenty-one and at a crossroads. Locate which sign Saturn is in right now and where it is in your chart, then see what their corresponding chapters have to tell you. You'll soon learn how to trace Saturn's progression in sync with your own evolution.

Every three-ish years, when Saturn changes sign, flip to the house of inquiry and get a sense of Saturn's specific plans for you. You do not need to read this book linearly or all at once. It is meant to be a reference, a guide, lived through and understood anew as you progress through your own cyclical metamorphoses.

A word of advice: You may be trying to make sense of one planet, one sign, one moment in your life because of what your birth chart dictates. But it's worth taking all these in as part of a larger whole rather than identifying with one or another. All the planets and signs are present within you, all the time. Think of the characters in *Sex and the City*; you could say that you are really a Samantha and certainly *not* a Carrie, but you'd be missing the bigger picture. You're all of them, and, as symbolic representatives, they're all a part of you. Similarly, the archetypes of astrology all represent different aspects of our global and interpersonal orbit.

I offer my interpretations on how Saturn impacts you. But it is my intention for you to start making sense of these archetypes in your own language. Read this book, and you'll be armed with the vocabulary and imagination to engage with forces of change, not in passivity but in creative collaboration.

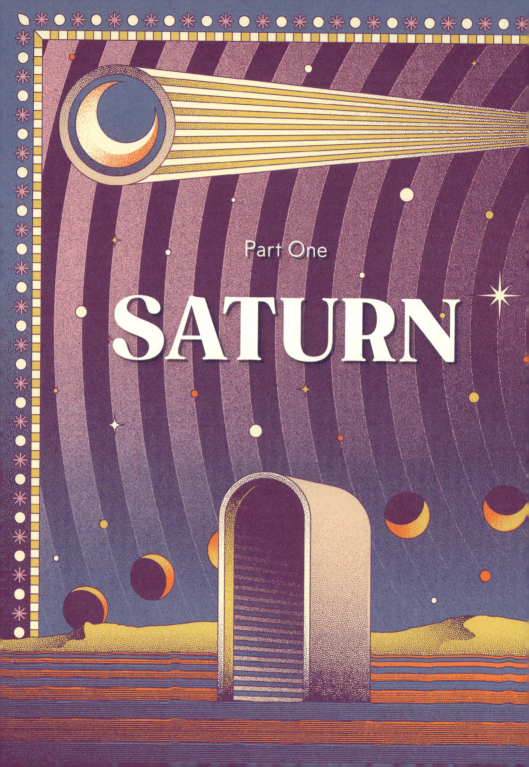

MEET YOUR TERMINATOR

The secret to life is meaningless unless you discover it yourself.
—W. Somerset Maugham, Of Human Bondage

At the start of all our favorite movies, our hero is something of a nobody: a farmboy, a waitress, a photographer for the high school yearbook. Inevitably, some catalyst will push the agenda of their evolution. Luke Skywalker wouldn't have gotten very far if his house hadn't been burned down. Sarah Connor would still be working in a diner if a Terminator or two hadn't forced her to start doing one-armed pull-ups. This crisis—which wakes us up, kicks us out of our old digs, and beats us into fighting shape—is of Saturn's design.

Saturn is our Terminator, an agent of fate sent to hunt you down until you're ready to face it. It has no moralistic imperative, nor any personal vendetta against you specifically, but, like it or not, it has come for you and will not relent until you stop running and fight back. Saturn's job is to bring you into focus, to align you with the path of highest efficiency. The cosmos has a rich and expansive plan for you; Saturn comes in to ensure that you stay on schedule with destiny. Often, blowing up your life is the easiest way to reset the clock.

Real pressure must be applied to assure lasting change. Each of us is held back by something: guilt, obligation, addiction, delusion, relationships, oppressive circumstances, or emotional baggage. We all want to make our dreams come true and live in the present moment, but expansion comes with sacrifice. Stakes get higher. We learn how to take care of ourselves, how to be accountable. This is growing up—Saturn's bread and butter. If you can meet Saturn as a partner, a cocreator, you will debut as strong, solid, and unkillable—the protagonist of a story that could only be your own. Are you in?

The nature of Saturn

Named after the gods of the Olympic pantheon, the planets embody different elements within our world and within ourselves. Their progression, from the sun all the way to Pluto, is an evolution of consciousness. In this saga, Saturn represents coming-of-age: responsibility, rules, structure, authority, boundaries, and consequences. Not necessarily a cheerful figure, but without Saturn's hard lines, we'd never take shape.

Until the confirmed discovery of Uranus in the late-eighteenth century, Saturn was thought to be the final planet in our solar system, the end of the line. And so Saturn represents limits and endings. Because the sun, Mercury, the moon, Venus, Mars, and Jupiter all move through the signs at a fast clip, we know them as the *personal* planets, their effects more immediate in the day-to-day. Uranus, Neptune, and Pluto (an essential planet in astrology, no matter how scientists classify it) are *generational*: They spend many years in each sign, affecting the global consciousness at large. Saturn, sitting in between the personal and generational, is the checkpoint planet, the bridge between the self and the universal.

Saturn's bodily correspondences are the skeleton and the teeth, its preferred metals are lead and iron, and its mineral is obsidian. Sensing a theme? Its associations are not soft or colorful, but hard and enduring. That which is weak or decayed will crumble. But what is hard and polished will endure for the long run.

Whether Saturn brings us into contact with literal death or the release of an old self, through rock bottom or a coming-of-age, the planet's currency is finitude. Whatever your life was, it's over now. In classical imagery, Saturn wields a scythe, ready to cut the grains down. But this grim reaper means not to deliver you to oblivion, but to hack away that which is already dead and make room for the next harvest. Monitoring figures, sums, and numbers, Saturn is the bookkeeper of the Milky Way, ensuring that the archetypal journey of the planets is on schedule, that none of us are lagging behind. If something isn't working up to standard, then an audit will be necessary.

Time is Saturn's fixation. Saturn takes twenty-eight years to complete an orbit around the sun, spending about three years in every sign. The zodiac tells its own story, of questions and ideas progressing through the ages. Saturn's three-ish-year eras put each sign's motives under a global reckoning, often registering in the realms of law, culture, and public discourse. A three-year time span can see institutions crumble, morals shift, and new social doctrines take shape.

Saturn *rules* Capricorn and Aquarius, the penultimate signs of the zodiac that mark the heart of the winter. Capricorn is the sign of the father figure and his duties: work, authority, planning for the mean seasons. Aquarius, co-ruled by the rebellious Uranus, employs Saturn's orderly methodology toward social progress, movements, and ideals. These two exemplify Saturn's passion to build structures of lasting value.

Saturn, or Kronos, is the father of the Olympic pantheon in Greco-Roman mythology. Fearing the prophesied succession of his heirs, he swallows them all, devouring them in his cavernous stomach. But Rhea, the mother of Saturn's children, tricks him into eating a stone in place of his son Jupiter. Growing into a formidable warrior, Jupiter returns to defeat Kronos (and force him to spit out the rest of the family). Inevitably, as always, son overthrows dad, and that's that—not a pretty painting of astrology's father archetype. Regardless of all Saturn's filicidal tendencies, he was and is celebrated in Roman culture. His reign is thought to be the golden age of Earth, before the complications of our messy gods and our own free will. Saturn carries the dual legacies of all fathers: the safety they provide and the power struggles to come. This is Father Time, the Heavenly Father, Don Corleone, or any great and powerful daddy who presides over our imagination.

Like gods taking human guise, planets often register as people. Saturn will likely incarnate in your life as a parent or authority figure. Just as Luke Skywalker faced Darth Vader, you must reckon with the ways you've avoided becoming your parents or fallen right into their worst behaviors. Saturn's endgame for you is absolute autonomy. To move with presence in the world, you'll have to learn to wield power, a prospect both dangerous and delicate. More often than not, your ability to take care of yourself, to stand on your own two feet, to be seen, is informed by your early conditioning. Saturn will shake the ancestral tree to its roots until you're ready to own the gifts and consequences of your upbringing, integrate the past, and act with agency now.

INTERPRETING SATURN

Astrology is a study of revolutions, but with Saturn, familial and societal life cycles are especially pronounced. Break Saturn's twenty-eight years into seven-year quadrants, and life's significant turning points are accounted for. Saturn puts us through trials and transitions to definitively mark a new chapter: You were someone's child; now you're someone's parent. You were the rebel; now you're the CEO. We identify these turning points, and the eras they precede, using the tools of astrology.

Before we engage with Saturn's complexities, we should consider how we "read" the planets and interpret their actions. As a planet moves through the heavens, it interacts with all the key players and celestial bodies, creating a unique meal especially catered to you—your birth chart. Here are the archetypes we employ to make meaning of your chart and your life.

The planets

There are ten planetary archetypes in our solar system and endless asteroids. Each acts with its own imperatives, representing parts of you or the system to which you belong. The planets are the substance, the content, the food, without which we'd be staring at empty dishware. Based on their positioning, the planets may pair well together or clash, but Saturn is always on the menu. If you can observe Saturn's engagements with the other planets, you can see what lies ahead.

The signs

Our solar system is divided into twelve signs, which can be thought of as fields of consciousness. The planets are constantly touring through these domains, shifting their modes of expression. In other words, if the planets are the food, the signs are the style of cooking. Each sign has its own elemental makeup and evolutionary purpose. Saturn's assignment in the earthy-diva sign Taurus will be vastly different from its work in the reactive air sign Gemini. Some planets take weeks to move through a single sign, while others can set up shop for decades at a time. Saturn's sign placement tells us the recipe, but we don't yet know the progression in which it will be served.

The birth chart

How did the planets land into the signs when you were born, and what can that tell us about you? To grasp your place in this larger unfolding saga, we use a birth chart, which looks like a compass, frozen in time the moment you were born. The chart is broken into twelve houses, which are like hours on a clock, each with its own meaning. We can interpret virtually all there is to know about you based on the positioning of the planets and signs in specific houses. To stretch the cooking metaphor to the point of breaking, this is the plating of the meal, without which we'd be eating delectable food off the kitchen floor.

The chart begins and ends at the nine o'clock point and travels counterclockwise. It launches with the *ascendant*, or rising sign, which is the sign breaking over the eastern horizon (dawn) the moment you were born. The ascendant lays out the exact positioning, down to the degree, of all the elements in your chart. Charts can be easily configured online, so long as one has their birth date, time, and location. You can pull up your chart for free on sites like Astro-Seek or on apps like CHANI. There are endless systems for configuring and arranging birth charts, which may set different planets in different houses. Remember what the Buddha says: Truth is what is useful. If something locks into place for you, follow it.

The houses

Like the epic of the zodiac, the birth chart is broken into twelve parts, each an essential crossing on the hero's journey of the planets. These are known as the *houses*, which are fixed in place for everyone and dictate which area of your life a planetary transit will impact. Each house has its own meaning and assignment: The fourth house deals with home and family, the seventh deals with relationships, etc. By calculating your birth chart, you can see where exactly the planets and signs fall on the houses for you specifically and witness the shape and scale of your personal astrological saga.

The houses correspond with the original order of the zodiac, so the first house will share attributes with Aries, the first sign, and the twelfth house will operate in a Piscean nature. But based on your birth time, any sign can fall on any house. That sign's directives will be applied to the house's specific range of focus.

Natal and transiting

Natal refers to the position of the planets the moment you were born. Your natal chart and natal planets are fixed and set forever. These provide us with essential information about who you are and what you're here to do.

When we consider the current position of the planets, we refer to them as *transiting*. So your natal Saturn may be in Pisces, if that's where it was when you were born. What does it mean if Saturn is, in this present moment, transiting through Gemini? Consider how the two are interacting, what kind of angle they are making, what the two signs say to or about each other. Depending on their interaction, transiting Saturn may be revealing natal Saturn's latent talents or challenging it to rethink its strategy. The frisson between transiting and natal planets sparks a dialogue between *now* and *then*. This is the language of change.

By viewing these factors as active elements and not stagnant qualifiers, you'll come to regard your chart and Saturn's presence in it as the greatest story ever told, one inviting your own interpretation and creative collaboration. It is not so much about locating your Saturn Return as it is about contemplating its part in a much bigger piece and recruiting the rest of the chart to add texture to your experience.

TRACKING SATURN

To understand where and how Saturn is registering in your life, we consider its placement. Which sign was it in the day you were born and at this very moment, and where are those signs in your personal birth chart? When you talk about your sign, you are referring to the sign that hosted the sun on the day you were born. We want to know where Saturn was on that same day. For example, when I was born, the sun was in Taurus, while Saturn was in Capricorn.

As Saturn spends three or so years in every sign, its broad assignments will apply to everyone in your generational cohort no matter what their sun signs are. Think about the experiences you share with everyone you went to high school with: You may have been a few grades apart, but you have the same cultural associations. I was born in 1990, when Saturn was in Capricorn (1988–1991), and like everyone else born within that three-year period, I showed up as the Berlin Wall fell and the World Wide Web came alive. When Saturn next returned to Capricorn (2017–2020), the Web had evolved into a corrupting political force. A global pandemic and economic crash toppled monoliths of authority. We had to wrestle with the same epochal themes we'd been born into. Consider Saturn's sign placement at your birth to make sense of your generation's objectives.

Nothing is ever as simple as it seems, and Saturn's progression through the signs is not always linear. Astrology is a *geocentric* study, which posits Earth as the center of the universe. Often, as Earth "catches up" to a planet, it produces an illusory effect in which the other planet moves backward. If you've ever been on a train and observed the car on the parallel track, you know this trippy feeling. This is what we call a *retrograde*, which acts as something of an archetypal backward lurch, review, or reintegration. Often, Saturn will tiptoe into a new sign before sliding back to its old digs for a few months more. For this reason, this book includes the specific dates of each of Saturn's sign transits so that you know exactly where it was when you were born and where it is this very day.

To understand Saturn's specific influence on you, we consider the birth chart. Different areas of the chart focus on different parts of your life: home, family, relationships, creativity, etc. By understanding where Saturn was when you were born or where it is now, we can stack up a lot of information on the lessons awaiting you. I was born with Saturn in my second house of earning and self-worth. When Saturn returned there, I had to deal with issues of invisibility, underearning, and codependence. As I write this chapter, Saturn has freshly entered my fourth house of home and family, leading me to lay down roots and forge a new way forward with my family.

Like any circle, the wheel of the birth chart can be broken up into four slices. Over Saturn's twenty-eight-year cycle, it will hit a new quadrant every seven years or so. As it comes to 90 or 180 degrees from its placement at the time of your birth, it makes a hard angle, spelling out an archetypal showdown. Call it a seven-year itch or just a shake-up, but in these periods, Saturn aims to put you back on track, into the life you were meant to live. These are your warning calls, reminding you to get yourself in gear before the big return is upon you. The effects of these checkpoints will depend on Saturn's sign and house placement.

Saturn's Angles

We mark Saturn's positioning using degrees, which are like minutes in an hour or tickers on a stopwatch. Each sign and house has 30 degrees, and Saturn moves about 12 degrees a year. When looking at one's chart, an astrologer considers the planets' current positions in the heavens in relation to their place in your birth chart. When transiting planets make angles to natal planets (the positioning of the planets when you were born), they set off critical periods of change. This may sound arbitrary, but astrologers have predicted the deaths of kings, down to the day, using angles and degrees.

An interaction among two or more of the planets is called an *aspect*, and its meaning is gleaned through angles. These can play out as collaborations or clashes, some of which can lead to gridlock, and others to positive propulsion forward. As we've established, Saturn takes about twenty-eight to thirty years to make a full revolution through the zodiac. But every seven years, transiting Saturn (i.e., currently on the move) will make some angle to its natal position in your chart (i.e., where it was when you were born).

Here's how they go down.

The Saturn square: approximate ages seven, twenty-one, thirty-six, fifty, sixty-five, seventy-nine

At 90 degrees, we encounter a square, or a challenge—something of a cosmic check-in, a seven-year closing point. Either you're bringing something to culmination or you're taking a left turn and starting anew. It's meant to integrate and expand your worldview, to pull you out of any traps you've fallen into these past few years.

The Saturn opposition: approximate ages fourteen, forty-three, seventy-two

Saturn is 180 degrees from its original position in your chart. This archetypal showdown inspires rebellion against forces you view to be constricting you. In your teen years, it's you against your parents. Come your forties, and certainly your seventies, you more or less stop caring what other people think and go your own way. Certainly, these can take the form of clichéd pubescent tantrums or midlife crises, but the call to dust off the old shouldn't be disregarded.

If you are experiencing a Saturn square or opposition, look to transiting Saturn's sign and house position, then consult the corresponding chapters in this book. The stakes and themes will be on the same track as those of a Saturn Return in the same arena.

Enough with the overture. Now we face the main event: the Return.

THE THREE SATURN RETURNS IN YOUR LIFE

When Saturn completes a full revolution—a Saturn Return—all hell breaks loose. Previous means of escape will be stripped away as you take a sobering accounting of your life so far. Face this period with humility, engaging with all your shortcomings and potentials, and you will indeed become Saturn, the master of your own fate. You will finally relinquish your role as center of the universe and, newly freed to be anybody or anything, find the role that is yours alone to fulfill. It's pretty trippy.

The term *Saturn Return* has two applications: one broad and one specific. We are studying what happens when Saturn comes back to its original position in your birth chart the moment you were born. For the specific application, Saturn will spend a week or so at that position before moving on. The exact Saturn Return acts as a climax in the three-year trial. Often, this is when the long-building breakup finally goes down, or when you pack your car and leave town for good. But just as often, something comes to synthesis under the surface. It's not always conscious, or cohesive, in the immediate. If you focus only on Saturn's exact return in your chart, it's like you're seeing only one tile and missing the whole mosaic. For all intents and purposes in this book, we refer more broadly to the *entire* time that Saturn is in the sign of its return—three-ish years—as your Saturn Return era.

My exact Saturn Return went down over the first few days of February 2020, then again in September of that year. These punctuated the story of my *entire* Saturn Return in Capricorn (December 2017–December 2020), the effects of which I felt—*unrelentingly*, I should say—every day of that three-year trial. Because Saturn retrogrades every year, it may hit its original degree in your chart multiple times, causing you to go through two or three Saturn Return events. It may feel like the cosmos is rubbing salt in the wound, but it's likely that something has yet to be resolved. Saturn has returned (again) to really seal the deal. Retrogrades give you another chance at processing and closure so that you can move on for good.

Here's how the returns will play out.

The first Saturn Return: approximate ages twenty-seven to thirty

This of course will be the star of the series, simply because we know so little about ourselves in our twenties and therefore have much to learn—and lose. Saturn has now completed its first revolution in your chart, signaling the definitive end of your childhood. That's not to say that at age twenty-seven you won't have experienced hard work, adversity, or achievement, but that *some* essential reconfiguration is necessary. Think of your favorite actress, who won an Oscar at age twenty-one, now discovering her true passion for activism in war-torn countries. In the scheme of things, you're still quite young, so a change in career, lifestyle, or religion is likely on the menu. Any self-sabotaging behaviors will come under fire, as will unhealthy familial attachments that keep one trapped in childish projections.

The second Saturn Return: approximate ages fifty-six to sixty

This is around the time when your favorite actress writes her memoirs, when the Mafia boss considers his successor, when empty nesters decide how they want to enjoy the next chapter of life. By this point, you have transitioned to the role of leader, in your family or at work, and have cleared the obstacles to authorship over your own life. Your relationship with your health has changed. You've likely lost a parent or loved one. What is important to you now? Are you ready to transition into a new role? This Saturn Return can produce a bitter old fart afraid to relinquish power or a charmed and curious adventurer ready to explore new horizons, enjoy life, and share what they've learned with the next generation.

The third Saturn Return: approximate ages eighty-four to ninety

And now, your favorite actress is ready to receive her lifetime-achievement award, surrounded by her progeny and admiring industry. This should be a celebration. I write this book as septuagenarians and octogenarians battle over a seat in the White House. That's not to say that with age you should give up and disappear, but if you're still trying to cling to power, you're in for a late and ugly awakening—Saturn has plans for you still. The transition to wise elder should be warm and enriching. You deserve respect, and to have your point of view honored, but you're ready to let the younger ones do the schlepping.

We have a firmer handle on Saturn's time frame and trajectory. Now begins the creative interpretation, in which we see how Saturn has applied its mission through each of the signs and what it has planned for you over the cycle to come.

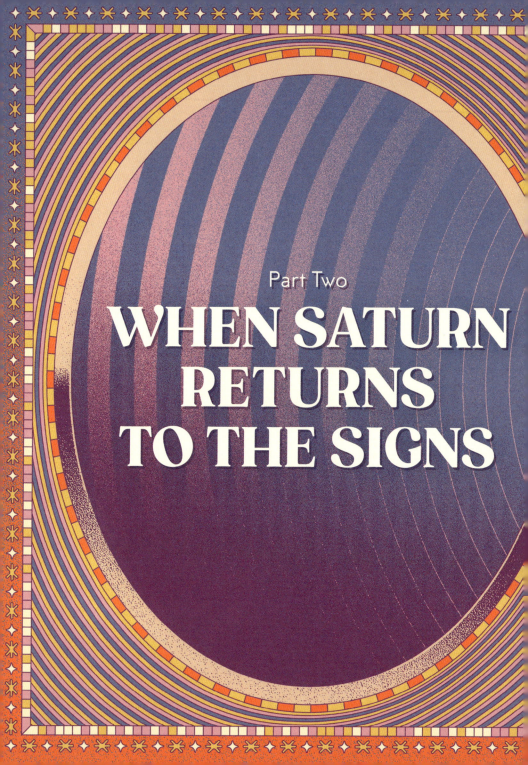

Part Two

WHEN SATURN RETURNS TO THE SIGNS

THE SIGNS

S aturn is the great renovator, changing form based on the zodiac sign it enters. The nature of its placements reveals the generational or collective work laid out before us. Saturn spends three or so years in every sign, commanding a cultural redefinition of its themes. These lengthy periods are necessary to mark irreversible change and reshape the sign's form for this moment. Though a Saturn generation only lasts a few years, those born under the same sign placement will wrestle with similar thematic issues.

Over the next twelve chapters, we will study Saturn's progression through the signs of the zodiac, zooming out to see how these stories have played out over the past century or so and what form we expect them to take in the revolution to come. By tracking Saturn's movement in the macro in our society, we make sense of its implications for the individual in the micro. You begin to witness your own evolution as part of a larger recurring cultural cycle.

Some key factors to note regarding signs and their effects for Saturn include elements, triplicities, and sign rulerships.

Elements

The twelve signs of the zodiac are divided into four elements:

FIRE SIGNS

Aries, Leo, and Sagittarius
Fire signs represent *creation*: action, conquest, drive, propulsion.

EARTH SIGNS

Taurus, Virgo, and Capricorn
Earth signs are the domains of *consolidation*: embodiment, ownership, value.

AIR SIGNS

Gemini, Libra, and Aquarius
Air signs correspond with *exchange*: dialogue, influence, ideas.

WATER SIGNS

Cancer, Scorpio, and Pisces
Water signs involve *connection*: blood, love, faith.

Triplicities

The zodiac corresponds to the four seasons of the year, with three signs in each season. Each seasonal trilogy has its own arc.

CARDINAL SIGNS

Aries, Cancer, Libra, and Capricorn
Cardinal signs launch the season and carry with them a drive to initiate. They are always on the move.

FIXED SIGNS

Taurus, Leo, Scorpio, and Aquarius
Fixed signs fall in the center of a season and embody its themes. Their function is not to *do*, but to *be*.

MUTABLE SIGNS

Gemini, Virgo, Sagittarius, and Pisces
Mutable signs end one season and phase us into another. They facilitate a transition between states.

The triplicities are arranged by 90- and 180-degree angles, which means that, for example, if Saturn is in one mutable sign, it will make key angles to the other three. If you were born with Saturn in Sagittarius, its arrival in fellow mutable sign Gemini, 180 degrees across the way, will trigger an important opposition for you.

Sign oppositions are worth noticing, as they'll help you view the zodiac as a whole rather than as twelve separate pieces. You can think of opposite signs as two sides of a coin, the motives of one directly informing the other. If Aries is about the self, Libra concerns others. But often, we can see ourselves only through the gaze of others, and so on. These oppositions, and the triplicities they form, reveal the connective thread of this tapestry.

Sign Rulerships

Every sign can be thought of as a collection of ideas. Each has a ruling planet, which acts like its emissary or champion. When a planet is in its home or *ruling* sign, its effects are most direct. When it occupies its opposite sign, 180 degrees away, it sets the same planet in its *detriment*, producing a battle of perspectives. Similarly, every planet has a sign in which it is *exalted*, or thriving, and across the way, in its *fall*, or misunderstood.

Saturn rules Capricorn and co-rules Aquarius with Uranus, is in detriment in Cancer and Leo, reaches exaltation when it hits Libra, and is fallen in Aries.

- **Transits through a ruling sign:** A Saturn transit in Capricorn and Aquarius—two signs concerned with big-picture governance, social movements, and planning for the future—will not necessarily be a cakewalk, but we can understand that the planet's mission is generally aligned with its home sign.

- **Transits through sign of detriment:** Capricorn's and Aquarius's opposite signs, respectively, are Cancer and Leo, where Saturn is in its detriment. While trying to run its audit, Saturn must deal with messy human sentimentality and more myopic points of view.

- **Transits through sign of exaltation:** Saturn is exalted in Libra, where it adores the Jane Austen game of social manners. It employs Libra's drive toward harmony to methodically reset the scales.

- **Transits through a sign in fall:** Across the way from Libra, Saturn is in its fall in the self-centered Aries. Saturn's system analysis feels limited in a sign with such an immediate point of view.

Even though Saturn may operate more efficiently in one sign over another, that does not indicate a better or worse placement. Wherever Saturn was located when you were born, it has a lifetime of work set out ahead for you.

When Saturn Returns to ♈

ARIES

Key Directives:
Drive, initiative, creation, conflict, sex

Dates:
March 20, 1908–May 18, 1910
December 14, 1910–January 21, 1911
April 25, 1937–October 17, 1937
January 14, 1938–July 5, 1939
September 21, 1939–March 19, 1940
March 3, 1967–April 29, 1969
April 6, 1996–June 8, 1998
October 25, 1998–February 28, 1999
May 24, 2025–August 31, 2025
February 13, 2026–April 12, 2028

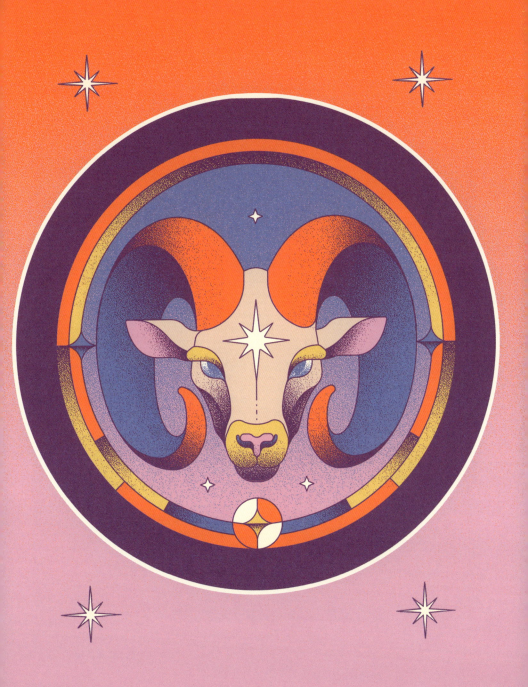

CHOOSE YOUR BATTLE, OR YOU WON'T SURVIVE THE WAR.

Saturn is in its fall in Aries, the sign that blasts off the zodiac, the atomic launch site of individuality, heroism, and conflict. Saturn is the lord of time, along with perspective, restraint, accountability. Youthful Aries, meanwhile, stomps in as the righteous superhero, its worldview simple: good versus evil, right versus wrong, me versus them. When Saturn returns to Aries, it will force you to hone your destructive urges and consider what you're fighting for.

Aries acts as the engine of the zodiac, containing within it enough sexual and creative firepower to propel us through the next eleven signs to come. Aries is ruled by Mars, the god of war, and for Saturn to cool down the inferno, it must first unleash a culture's aggressions, as if bringing an illness to a raging fever.

Saturn comes to Aries in times of great social upheaval, when the war god inspires youth revolution and international warfare. The 1937–1940 edition was something of a global boiling point, as young men raised in the shame and destitution of World War I took up arms once again to reclaim purpose and masculinity—no matter the cost.

Saturn's tour of the late '60s was a time of legendary integrated activism—and horrific reprisals, with the assassinations of Martin Luther King Jr., John F. Kennedy, and Robert F. Kennedy, among many others. France was embroiled in protests, thirty-two African countries gained independence from their colonial overlords, and protests exploded worldwide against American aggression in Vietnam.

Come the late '90s, as war in the Congo and Kosovo left millions dead and displaced, male animus warped and curdled stateside. These years saw the explosion of exploitative internet porn, the debut of the *Girls Gone Wild* franchise, and the dark lead-up to the Golgothan mud pits of Woodstock '99. School shootings were just beginning to shift from phenomenon to epidemic. The days of grunge and soulful R & B were over. Something violent was brewing.

All fevers must rage before they can get better, but with these global meltdowns comes great tragedy, as the lives of soldiers, artists, thinkers, and luminaries are lost in the fire. Many pledge themselves to join a fight, only to have their passions exploited on the front line. Viewing themselves as victims, they will be too easily conscripted, going down like stormtroopers or Orcs.

So how do you engage? Walk away? It is not Saturn's intention to make all of us into pacifists, to sit out the storm and do nothing. Both destruction and creation are necessary parts of the cycle, but Saturn would rather you be a part of the latter. Now is when we learn to choose our battles.

As a global transit affecting us all, Saturn's 2025 arrival in Aries will test our algorithmically programmed impulse to comment first and ask questions later, to identify with prescribed definitions before discovering one's own place. Global conflict will draw new battle lines, and many who have acted on moralistic reflex will have their compasses rattled by the messy reality of war. As the tired leaders of the old world are finally put out to pasture, a new class, undergoing their Saturn Return in Aries, will take the reins. Saturn would like for you to rise among them.

But we'll need you to be able to last the whole war, not die on a single, likely unnecessary hill. Consider your relationship to conflict and cancellation, especially in the realm of social media, a synthetic war zone that feeds off righteous indignation. That's not to say that all discourse spurred on by social media is unwanted; in many cases, they serve the Aries call to fight injustice. But those experiencing their Saturn Returns in Aries will be forced to consider the "stands" they've taken and what they've really accomplished, if they were personally offended by something or are yelling by proxy, and if their actions did more harm than good when all is said and done. Each of us, over and over again, must ask ourselves what it is we are really angry about.

Your evolution begins when you acknowledge that you may not be the protagonist of the piece. Then, inevitably, comes the realization that some stories have neither heroes nor villains—just sick, sad, scared, lonely people doing their best. This may invalidate your entire romantic history, because, unfortunately, most adult relationships involve mutual harm and benefit. If you have gone through every coupling of your twenties believing yourself to be the victim, you're in for a rude awakening when you start therapy at age twenty-eight. Come to this place of ambivalence, and you'll know freedom: Here's what they did, and here's what you did. Now we begin the process of forgiveness, and we can really move forward.

Such a humbling silence often comes by way of humility or disenchantment. You realize that the cronies you kept with don't really align with your values, and that the causes you aligned with feel like relics of the past. And you start to see yourself differently. Once upon a time, it was you against the world, here to liberate the suburbs of your upbringing from the tyranny of your parents or your high school principal. But as you take account of the battles you've waged and begin the brutal but essential process of forgiving yourself and the people in your life, the casting of heroes and villains is reshuffled.

A Saturn Return in Aries delivers the humility essential to make you a champion, not a chump. By cultivating accountability, working in coalition with people of differing perspectives, choosing which fight to engage in, and learning the value of intentional inaction, one may transcend Padawan status and become a calm, collected Jedi Master.

Your Saturn Return in Aries represents a hero's awakening; you will realize what it is that you alone can do, the point of view that defines you as unique and essential to this new cycle and the cycles to come. But to cultivate this originality, you'll have to step out of the insanity and find your own way.

Aries is the sign of individualism and originality, both of which are easily compromised when one engages in irrational reactivity. But those born to Saturn in Aries are great minds who go their own way, devising new means of engagement with a changing world, including:

- Early-twentieth-century activist and mystic Simone Weil
- Revolutionary scientist Albert Einstein
- Holocaust-era liberator Oskar Schindler
- Pioneering "Prince of Soul" Marvin Gaye
- Pakistani Nobel Peace Laureate Malala Yousafzai

With the old wars finished and forgiven, Saturn can set you to the real revolutionary labor, which requires deep listening, collaboration, empathy, and flexibility. You're no longer living in the last cycle, but a patient and considerate builder of the new world.

In the sign of creation, the master architect Saturn is looking to construct great and lasting institutions. After completing a thirty-year cycle, we can finally look ahead. In the late '30s, Superman, Shazam, and Batman came swooping in under this transit, soon to become the gods of the postmodern age. In the late '60s, the Beatles, the Rolling Stones, Jimi Hendrix, and Aretha Franklin took music into unknown frontiers. The end of the twentieth century brought us the high-kicking Spice Girls and Destiny's Child, along with the complex women of *Buffy the Vampire Slayer*, emissaries of a new credo called Girl Power. These symbols were active and alive, and were able to engage with and inspire the rising generations.

Creation over destruction. You witness others going down in flames, casting themselves as heroes in social media feuds that won't mean much in a few years' time. But you're invested in something that delights and inspires you, with the possibility to start a new story. You have your own point of view, which you're excited to share but doesn't have to be inflicted on others. With Saturn's return to Aries comes the possibility of a new beginning: Who do you want to be? What do you want to do?

When it's time for your second Saturn Return in Aries, you may be shocked to find yourself in the role of mentor and not protagonist. Once upon a time, you were wild, ferocious, and daring; many of your previous identities and careers were defined by streaks of hyperreactivity to the moment. Now the grooves have set in. Those causes that inflamed you in your youth are as relevant as ever, but this time, you have the wisdom to know your place in the battle plan. But that doesn't mean the fight is over. A second Saturn Return in Aries does not necessarily spell out diminishment or hermitage. Often, it allows for a clear and direct approach to one's lifework: a fifty-eight-year-old Dostoyevsky publishing *The Brothers Karamazov* in 1880 or a sixty-year-old Tina Turner leading the highest-grossing concert tour of 2000. The drama is done, which means we can really get to work.

Aries represents the spring, new life, and the awakening of one's life forces. Those undergoing their second and third Saturn Returns in the sign of virility and vitality are perhaps at greatest risk of becoming cliché, seeking fountains of renewed vigor through young lovers, sports cars, and the miracles of cosmetic surgery. Look, if it doesn't harm anyone, who cares? But the youth you *should* preserve, which Saturn will store in a vault for you until you're ready, is the optimism that once made the world seem new and verdant to you, the belief that change is possible and that you could be an essential agent of its delivery, and the knowledge that conflict in collaboration can be creative.

You're not the victim or the hero. You're nobody. Embrace that silence so that you can be recruited. Saturn wants you available and open-minded for the next great idea or collaboration. Now that you're not in opposition to the world, you can actually become a part of it.

When Saturn Returns to ♉
TAURUS

Key Directives:
Consolidation, embodiment, agency, wealth

Dates:
May 18, 1910–December 14, 1910
January 21, 1911–July 8, 1912
December 1, 1912–March 26, 1913
July 5, 1939–September 21, 1939
March 19, 1940–May 8, 1942
April 29, 1969–June 18, 1971
January 9, 1972–February 21, 1972
June 8, 1998–October 25, 1998
February 28, 1999–August 9, 2000
October 15, 2000–April 20, 2001
April 12, 2028–June 2, 2030

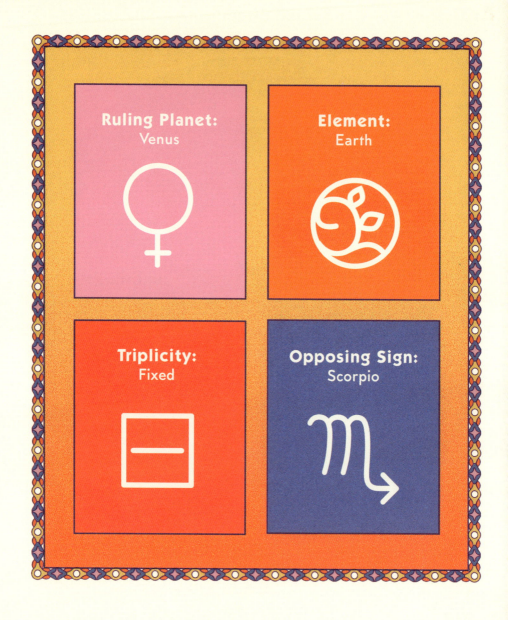

MAKE PEACE WITH YOUR SMALLNESS.

And so, on some such day of the week, God created Man in his image. From then on, in the Garden of Eden, we had our marching orders: to embrace our total incarnation as vessels of the divine. But somewhere along the way, we got confused about the chain of command.

If Aries represents the big bang, the cataclysmic launch of life, then Taurus takes us from raw creation to inherent design. We are no longer planting the seeds but trimming Eden's topiary. This is the sign of raw embodiment, of taking agency over our bodies and destinies. As a sign, its currency *is currency*: This is what I am, this is what I have, this is what I'm worth. With such declarative confidence at stake, no sector of the zodiac has yielded more divas, directors, or dictators than Taurus. As it happens, Saturn doesn't fancy competition for supreme intergalactic dominator. And so, when Saturn returns to Taurus, you'll have to stop playing God and embrace your small part in creation.

It's one thing to view yourself as the center of the world—we all do at some point—but quite another to try to remake the world *to our liking*, to have it reflect our tastes and sensibilities. Those born to Saturn in Taurus make up a long line of ego projectors, sucking us into delusory vortexes of their own self-conception:

- L. Ron Hubbard invented his own religion.
- Alexander the Great conquered the known world, to be unified under his vision.
- Liberace had his pianos bejeweled to match his coats.

But no matter how great the talent or vision, no one is above anyone else.

It can't have been easy, being the first occupants in the Garden of Eden. When Adam was introduced to his mate, he must have been confused. *If she's not me, then who is she?* It all comes down to the identification—or misidentification—of trying to see ourselves reflected in others and coping poorly when they break from our patterning. Saturn-in-Taurus eras are boom periods for racial warfare and genocide, including the beginning of the Holocaust, which saw the Taurean drive for control taken beyond authoritarianism. This order of fascists enforced a comprehensive aesthetic plan, which could not allow for anyone deemed imperfect. There could be no other. It could only be us—or, really, *me*. When Saturn returns to Taurus in 2028, the dangerous science of gene editing will come to a head, as our obsession with *optimization* is inflicted on the unborn.

Taurus's avatar is the bull, a beast not known to budge easily. That indomitable, indefatigable determination can be a boon, as celebrated by the Saturn-in-Taurus Barbra Streisand belting out "Don't Rain on My Parade" on a moving barge in *Funny Girl*. Read enough axioms about "staying true to you," and you'll believe obstinacy to be a virtue and compromise a failure. But the iron planet needs to keep the machine moving. No part can stay stuck in its own place.

The rising Saturn-in-Taurus generation (in 2028–2030), born in the technological boom of the 1998–2000 transit, has the power to design a new reality, and their will, like Barbra's, is uncompromising. Via access to unlimited information and resources, they can curate holistic, inclusive, expansive fields of art and perspective. They have grown up choosing their own digital avatars, editing selfies, and perceiving the world through endless kaleidoscopic phone filters. But what happens when we can't customize to our own perfection? Saturn wants you to develop the patience and flexibility to adapt so that you don't throw a tantrum when the planet doesn't spin at your command.

As this generation experienced its early-twenties-age Saturn square in Aquarius (2020–2023), classrooms and university seminars erupted. Students have since taken hold of curricula, demanding warnings for content they deem upsetting or offensive, setting the terms for what they can and will be exposed to. The young Taurean bulls should be celebrated for stomping through the static of their forebears, for challenging the status quo, for demanding to be heard. They have the extraordinary will to declare their identities, their desires, their selfhood to the world. Lacking in this design, however, is that—once in a while—it behooves us to be challenged, or enlightened, or even dazzled, by the unknown, the abject, the uncanny.

As you come closer to your first complete face-off with Saturn, you'll likely have to reflect on those missed opportunities to learn, to listen, to bend, to change. As they say in *A Course in Miracles*: "I do not perceive my own best interests." That's a tough one to swallow, and I say that as the most bullheaded of Taureans. Throughout my twenties, I knew what I wanted for myself: to write comic books and screenplays. Nothing else mattered. The signals that kept coming my way that were leading me toward my true path—they had to be irrelevant. But as new crises forced me to adapt and depend on others, and unexpected joy came in from a life I had not chosen, I had to concede: Maybe this—whatever *this* was—was it, rather than some endgame that was keeping me stuck in the future.

When Saturn first returns to Taurus, it will strip you of your illusory claims to authority, rendering meaningless any self-projections you once considered to be definitive. You are no longer the dictator of your living room, Orc Lord of a multiplayer online kingdom, or guerilla commander of the college dining hall. So who are you? Consider what it is that you value in yourself: those gifts or lessons that have come through experience and often humiliation. These will be more significant guideposts on your path than any of the limits or definitions you've placed on yourself thus far.

On a microscopic and more manageable level, how are you to cut the feed on the projection of your distorted reality? You'll need reflection from a two-sided mirror, accountability, and trustworthy voices of dissent that can help you see your blind spots. You will slowly and painfully train yourself to recognize those instances when you're upset not over any external issue, but because you feel out of control, scared, and confused. *That*, Saturn can work with. You won't have to take it out on the world if you can sit with it yourself.

We've discussed how Saturn will expose Taurean issues of myopic entitlement in all of us, but if your problem set is on the opposite end of the spectrum, if you've played the role of doormat, "going with the flow" in fear of claiming your voice, don't think Saturn won't be coming for you. Many of us who grew up in the blast radius of the narcissistic, self-indulgent, and grandiose believe that by staying small, we won't risk becoming the tyrants who crushed us. Saturn will introduce crises of decision and direction, in which you are forced to choose, to elect, to take up space.

By the end of your first Saturn Return, you will have come into that destined role of star power, centrality, or diva-dom—but not in the way you thought. This time, you're here to collaborate, to receive and apply feedback from your producers in the recording studio. You know who you are, but that doesn't mean you're stuck in yourself. You can embark and change with the tides rather than drown on a fixed course.

When Saturn returns in your midfifties, you're by now the boss—and not the boss baby of your late twenties. Unfortunately, with age, we tend to become more obdurate, more inflexible, more entitled. As a creative master, you will have to evolve—to adapt to new technologies, to learn from the next generation, to shift from lead actor to director. How will your contributions—and this includes your children—exceed you? How will they outlive you? You are not being forced into an early retirement—the Saturn-in-Taurus Hayao Miyazaki completed his masterpiece *Spirited Away* (which would go on to be the highest-grossing film in Japanese history for twenty years) during his second Saturn Return. But to think big picture, to have your work hit the world on a scale unforeseen, will require a sacrifice of selfhood.

Bulls have been worshipped in nearly every civilization for eons; the golden calf caused Moses a bit of trouble while he was working on the whole "one god" project. Idols have power. When Saturn enters the bull's domain, we see the genesis of unkillable, ever-sterling new monoliths: Pinocchio, Bugs Bunny, Wonder Woman, and even the Starbucks mermaid all emerged during Saturn-in-Taurus periods. These icons will endure long after their creators' names are forgotten. They no longer belong to the people who made them, but to the universal imagination, to all who register and identify with them.

If you are to create a life, a symbol, a movement, or a moment, it will inevitably surpass you. You will have to make peace with your smallness: You are the fertilizer but not the garden. In your brief time here, you deserve to be seen, affirmed, and certainly well paid for what you do. But in the end, it's not about you.

When Saturn Returns to ♊

GEMINI

Key Directives:
Experience, experimentation, dialogue

Dates:
July 8, 1912–December 1, 1912
March 26, 1913–August 24, 1914
December 8, 1914–May 11, 1915
May 8, 1942–July 19, 1944
June 18, 1971–January 9, 1972
February 21, 1972–August 1, 1973
January 7, 1974–August 18, 1974
August 9, 2000–October 15, 2000
April 20, 2001–June 3, 2003
June 2, 2030–July 15, 2032

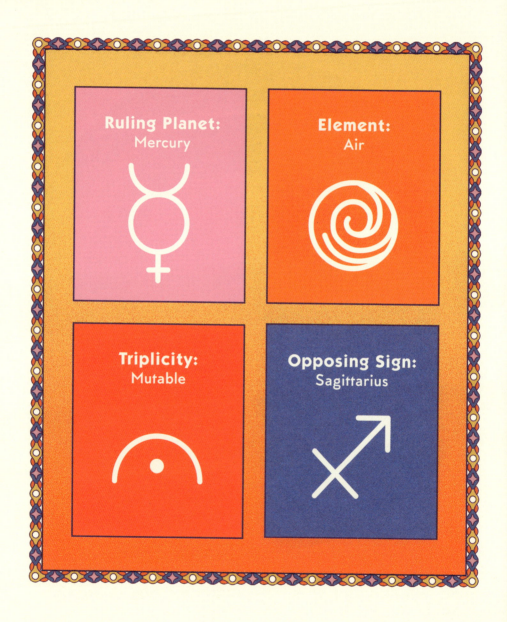

LET GO OF THE EXTREMES AND EMBRACE THE LONG GAME.

♊

Welcome to Cosmic Consciousness: The Teen Years. If we must reduce the zodiac to developmental stages, then Gemini, the third sign, falls somewhere in the adolescent phase of development. The twins represent polarities, opposites, and extremes; the lesson of this sign is to find balance somewhere in between. Saturn, the planet of consistency and function, will reveal your place at the stable center, no matter how severe the circumstances are around you. When Saturn returns to Gemini, you'll leave behind chaos and embrace longevity.

As evidenced by the time you totaled your mom's minivan or bleached your own hair orange, sometimes you can only learn by testing extremes. This is what teenagers do. They discover themselves in opposition, doing everything their parents say not to. They need to see what happens when they lick dry ice, stick their hands over the gas burner, ingest substances that are neither legal nor potable. In the cycle of culture, boundaries need to be pushed. New technologies are meant to be explored.

Saturn-in-Gemini periods always take us over the edge so that we may learn our limits. Saturn's twentieth- and twenty-first-century transits to the twins' domain are: the assassination of Archduke Franz Ferdinand, known as the "powder keg" that launched World War I (during the 1912–1915 return to Gemini); the development of the atom bomb by J. Robert Oppenheimer in Los Alamos, New Mexico, over the early-'40s edition; and September 11th and the ensuing "War on Terror" come the new millennium. Too much, too far, too fast.

Of course, these developments were at the hands of a very privileged few, but they represent a collective surrender to stoked anxieties, fears, and passions. It's been said that the internet, as of the writing of this book, is only in its adolescence, a period of reactivity and volatile mood states. If social media indeed reflects some version of interplanetary united consciousness, the hive mind needs to drink a green juice and take a breather. Saturn wants you to observe the situation and judge from a safe vantage point—not lose your mind.

This discernment will be critical come 2030 (as Elon Musk enters his second Saturn Return!). The reaper will have his scythe ready to shred whatever delusive, overblown fads we've invested in. Can you think of any technologies that could use a little regulation? More personally, are there any political movements, online communities, value systems, or practices that may feel limited to this moment, reactive to outside stimuli but not grounded in anything? I can think of a couple hundred, give or take.

We've discussed the manic intensity these eras bring, but those born to Saturn in Gemini will be no strangers to the fervor of adolescence. Some Saturn generations only begin to rebel, to exceed expectations, to take in all that life has to offer *after* their first return. For the Gemini cohort, it feels like the opposite. Those experiencing their first Saturn Return in Gemini may be surprised to find their lives cooling down, and for once not blowing up. You may not recognize yourself outside the polar vortex.

By age twenty-eight, you may feel as though you've done it all. Oasis front man Liam Gallagher had already played the biggest show of his life at age twenty-three; Monica Lewinsky had lived through the worst the '90s had to offer before she was twenty-five; and, at the time of this writing, Billie Eilish has two Oscars and nine Grammys. Rounding out the list of precocious Saturn in Geminis are Winona Ryder, Olivia Rodrigo, Greta Thunberg, and the

Notorious B.I.G. So what happens to the young provocateur when childhood comes to a swift and severe end? What happens when a Beatle or a Spice Girl gets old? Where do you go from here?

There are a few turns this sort of Saturn Return can take, and, based on readings with a small but vocally macabre subsection of my clientele, it behooves me to mention the "27 Club," which includes Jimi Hendrix, Jim Morrison, Janis Joplin, Brian Jones—all born with Saturn in Gemini, none enduring beyond its first return. Great artists who departed too soon and will always be remembered like the Greek heroes slain in battle: forever young and beautiful.

Be careful with this one. We live in a culture that romanticizes our salad days, before we are supposedly shackled with responsibility, inevitably sagging into the deflated armchairs our fathers once occupied, the stained aprons of put-upon mothers. The polarity is creeping in now. Youth is glorious, adulthood is punishing. Of course, this divide is illusory, and if you're still clinging to the fear of becoming your parents or having your youth ripped away from you, then you will be subject to some (hopefully metaphorical) version of the "death" the end of our twenties heralds.

With Saturn's help, you can experience youthful discovery at any age, without pushing yourself over the edge. One of the many gifts awaiting you at the end of a Saturn Return is the prospect of sustainable fun. It's why sex in your thirties is such a blast: Now that you can be trusted to get a regular STD test, identify your codependency issues, and even buy your own dinner, you can just get on with it and have a good time.

This being the sign of extremes, you may be delivered—eventually—to this harmonious neutral state only after going through a deep and devastating spin cycle. You may get everything you ever wanted—or, really, *thought* you wanted—only to have it taken away in one fell swoop. Observe the Ragnarök of your dreams, realized then dashed, and you'll begin to see one constant in the maelstrom: you.

At stake in all the chaos is the possibility of peace. What if, freed from a life of reaction, you could experiment, vibe, channel the currents between the tuning fork, the symbol of Gemini? This isn't a calling restricted to the Saturn Return period, but indeed a lifelong invitation toward reinvention. Gemini's highest vibration is ambivalence, which can be disenchanting but also liberating. Move through your first Saturn Return, and you get to experience true versatility, as evidenced by these Saturn in Geminis:

- Freed of his obligation to Beatledom, George Harrison could explore and embody his spirituality through music.
- Gwyneth Paltrow dropped the ingenue image and shellacked on heavy eyeliner to play the acidic Margot in *The Royal Tenenbaums* in 2001.
- Snoop Dogg hosts TV potlucks with Martha Stewart. Need I say more?

Gemini doesn't want you to be one thing or another, but to be a conduit, a neutral container of whatever happens next.

Generally, we think of the first Saturn Return (in any sign) as the time of lessons learned through catastrophe, but the older you get, the more power you wield, and the stakes only get higher. Apparently, you can make plenty of mistakes at any age. Richard Nixon won presidential reelection by a landslide and resigned in disappointment—within his second Saturn Return in Gemini in the early '70s. George Lucas released *Star Wars*: Episode II *Attack of the Clones*, the ambitious second installment of his *Star Wars* prequels, in 2002, during his second Saturn Return in Gemini. Talk about going overboard.

As we saw with the development of the atomic bomb and the ignition of World War I, there must have been a moment, in all these instances, when someone could have stopped and measured their actions. Just because you can take Yoda, a puppeteering triumph par excellence, and replace him with a computer-generated model doesn't mean you should. Gemini's ambivalence is indeed a spiritual calling; it requires one to choose their moment. That's not to say that, as you come into your midfifties or even eighties, you shouldn't take risks. Quite the opposite. If, say, you're president of the United States, your job is going to require fast action, and it could be argued that Nixon did a lot of good along with the bad. But all three Saturn Returns demand that the actor holds themselves separate from the extreme choices before them. The world will always be loud. It's on you to dial down the volume.

Saturn will force the question: Where are *you* in all this noise? Were you a consumer, a dupe, a firestarter, a reactionary? Your teen years are truly finished, and with adulthood comes expansive, often terrifying, space and the thrilling possibility of doing nothing rather than blowing it all to pieces.

When Saturn Returns to ♋ CANCER

Key Directives:
Security, nourishment, strength, a sustained future

Dates:
August 24, 1914–December 8, 1914
May 11, 1915–October 17, 1916
December 8, 1916–June 25, 1917
July 19, 1944–August 2, 1946
August 1, 1973–January 7, 1974
August 18, 1974–September 16, 1975
January 14, 1976–June 4, 1976
June 3, 2003–July 16, 2005
July 15, 2032–August 27, 2034
February 16, 2035–May 12, 2035

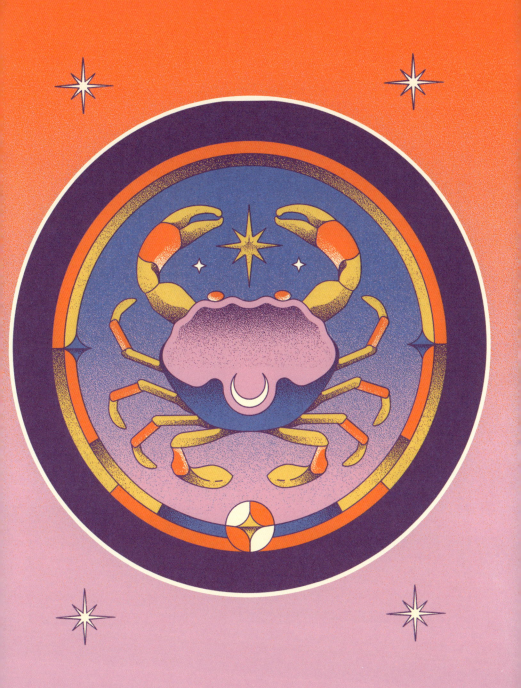

OWN IT AND LEAVE IT BEHIND.

♋

Cancer is the sign of security, home, and safety. Not incidentally, it is also the sign of the mother, ruling the mammary glands, passing onto us the story of our family, our traditions, our place in this world. One way or another, our mothers instill in us a sense of belonging. They give us a body so that we may feel safe in it. But how often does that plan go off without a hitch, and what do we do to overcompensate, to prove that we're big and strong and can't be hurt? When Saturn returns to Cancer, you'll have to own your vulnerability, or suffocate under the burden of your defense mechanisms.

Saturn rules Capricorn, the sign of the father and Cancer's opposite. In Capricorn, Saturn trades in cold hard facts: Here's how much Dad earned at the office so that we can keep the lights on. But because Saturn is in its fall in the sign of the crab, it finds the language of emotional stability to be nebulous. And so, when Saturn returns to Cancer, it examines the deeper needs that weren't met, all the way back through our childhoods, the fears our parents failed to face for us. Nowhere is truly safe. No matter how hard we try or how titanic we make ourselves, we can, at any time, be broken. Of all Saturn's cruel lessons, that one may be the biggest pain in the ass.

George W. Bush was reelected during his second Saturn Return in Cancer (2003–2005). The word *security* was everywhere in those days, used as a basis for a lot of retaliatory, dangerous behavior. Phones were tapped, armies were deployed, threats were made. Of course, this was all to cover up the real truth: We'd been hurt badly, and there was nobody to kiss the boo-boo and make it better. How would history have been different had we stopped looking for weapons of mass destruction and instead sat down and dealt with our grief?

In addition to Bush, Saturn in Cancer has yielded iconic and authoritative leaders overcompensating for their vulnerabilities: Napoleon Bonaparte, Elizabeth I, and Donald Trump. Harry Truman authorized the detonation of atom bombs on Hiroshima and Nagasaki during the World War II edition of Saturn in Cancer (1944–1946). Margaret Thatcher was first elected as British prime minister during Saturn's mid-'70s tour of the crab. As the first woman in such a seat of power in the United Kingdom, Thatcher was the perfect incarnation of the Cancerian provider, down to the uncrackable shell. But inevitably, her hard-line run was viewed as a failure of Cancer's primary imperative: to ensure everyone gets fed. And though Bonaparte's actual height is now debated by historians, the idea of his titular complex rings true: How many lands do you have to conquer, how many people have to die, so that you may mask your vulnerabilities with threats of violence and control?

Whether you preside over an empire or a studio apartment, and whether you're going through your Saturn Return in Cancer or not, this transit will make you consider what gives you a sense of security. It may be your body, your doorman, your family, your values. This is all rather abstract to Saturn, so it will want to pick it apart, like my mother putting her reading glasses on to see what's in her salad. Change is a definite during a Saturn Return, which means that you need to feel safe in yourself to face whatever comes next.

Where this gets complicated are the damages from long ago that don't immediately register but have tilted and warped all your choices thus far. With the help of a therapist or a well-stickered journal, you will think back to when you did not feel safe, or loved, or cared for, and how it still spurs you on, causing you to act out (or, in my case, to play out the abandonment, over and over again, like a bad movie on an international flight).

I'm not suggesting that Saturn is going to take away your penthouse just because you haven't processed the trauma of your Bat Mitzvah. But if you're putting on a show, huffing and puffing to prove something, taking up space to feel big, you're in for a crash. The bigger the car, the worse the damage come collision time.

Facing the false binary of strength and vulnerability, it's easy to forget that they're one and the same. Many of my Cancer clients don't fully realize the power of their sign. At our first reading, they'll hesitantly tell me that they're weak and watery. Yeah, right. The Cancer mother archetype is the great crone of the tribe, the one who has lived through all seasons and cycles: pain and joy, creation and devastation. I've seen crabs hanging on to the breakwater—nothing can make those suckers budge, at least not in the last four hundred million years. To endure and even command the tempests requires tremendous power. But you must have the courage to face the storm.

To step into your destiny, to command the full force of the ocean, you'll have to let Saturn break you open. You must do what they do at the crab shack: tie on a bib, crack apart the shell, and get to the juicy insides. People who work the twelve steps of recovery programs must own up to insanities and coping mechanisms, to the things we do to cover up some primal wound—that way of making your voice deep around your big brothers, that career ambition that has become your personality, that fixation on narcissists who will never really love you. You're going to have to own it and someday leave it behind, so you can move to the level of cosmic awareness.

The good news? Those who break free become gods. The Saturn-in-Cancer lineup includes Debbie Harry, Lauryn Hill, Liza Minnelli, Lil' Kim, Edith Piaf, M.I.A., Alanis Morissette, and Carly Simon. During their mid-'70s Saturn Returns in Cancer, Dolly Parton debuted "Jolene" and became a solo act, leaving behind Porter Wagoner, and Cher ended her marriage with Sonny Bono and launched her own show. Come her second Saturn Return (2003–2006), Cher launched the first of many farewell tours, at that point the most successful tour by a woman in history.

In their own ways, all these icons express: This is who I am, this is where I've been, this is what I've come through. The first Saturn Return in Cancer isn't just three years of weeping. It's about owning your shell and leaving it behind. Once free of that persona, or person, that you relied on for a false sense of safety, you're unleashed.

By the time of your second and third Saturn Returns in Cancer, you will have built the house or the institution. You are the parent. Many of us have wrestled with an iron patriarch or matriarch in the family, that overlord who can't take a joke, their progeny sneaking out back to smoke a joint before receiving another lecture. If you have hardened your heart in order to become the boss, changes in circumstance will force you to let go. When we experience grief or changes in our health, we find ourselves unexpectedly leaning on others, bursting into tears at the dinner table, not sweating the small stuff. Give in to it. You don't really have a choice.

Because the alternative—namely, masculine bravado—hasn't done much net good for the human race. You may be leader of the free world, but if you can only trade in hard aggression, you'll miss out on the love of your people. Your so-called thick skin doesn't frighten Saturn. But your beating, broken, bleeding heart? That'll send it running to the next solar system. The infinite power within you is meant to be owned and embraced, not proclaimed and enforced. Only by affirming your humanity—and all its shortcomings—can you truly claim immortality.

When Saturn Returns to ♌
LEO

Key Directives:
Creativity, leadership, dignity

Dates:
October 17, 1916–December 8, 1916
June 25, 1917–August 11, 1919
August 2, 1946–September 18, 1948
April 2, 1949–May 29, 1949
September 16, 1975–January 14, 1976
June 4, 1976–November 16, 1977
January 4, 1978–July 26, 1978
July 16, 2005–September 2, 2007
August 27, 2034–February 16, 2035
May 12, 2035–October 16, 2036
February 11, 2037–July 8, 2037

TAKE UP SPACE AND TAKE YOURSELF SERIOUSLY.

You've got to give it to fire signs: They know how to keep things simple. I can spend hours interpreting the arcana of Scorpio-star lore or explaining the Christian metaphors at stake in Piscean consciousness. But sometimes, no explanation is required: Leo is the sign of star power. When I inform my Leo clients of their divine entitlement, they either bask in their glory—naturally—or cower in denial. "What makes me so special? I work the X-rays at the airport!" Honey, get into it. When Saturn returns to Leo, you'll have to step all the way into the light and heal the pain that it exposes.

As Sylvester once belted, in a falsetto that is probably echoing through the Andromeda Galaxy by this point, *everybody* is a star. No human life passes without generating, transmitting, or refracting the light of the divine; even if your name will be forgotten within three generations (or, in all likeliness, sooner), you *will* have commanded some influence, left some legacy. What shape and scale your impact registers is between you and—you guessed it—Saturn.

Leo is the king of the zodiac, like the lion is the king of the jungle. Historically, a monarch is the crown and the crown is the monarch; they embody the kingdom and serve as its divine effigy. If they are healthy, regal, and resplendent, then so must be their people. Leo is in all our charts, meaning that we all embody something bigger than ourselves. During your first Saturn Return, Saturn's fixation on longevity, when matched with Leo's embrace of kingly resonance, is meant to align you with your own noble mission.

Over Saturn-in-Leo periods, we see new modes of self-expression command the culture. Our understanding of world leaders and celebrities, and what they inspire in us, shifts with the politics and technologies of the time. Those born to Saturn's late-'40s tour of Leo came of age during the renaissance of rock 'n' roll, when the pretty people on television suddenly went raw and radical. By the time of their late-'70s Saturn Returns in Leo:

- Freddie Mercury and Queen would debut "Bohemian Rhapsody";
- Stevie Nicks would release, with Fleetwood Mac, the definitive *Rumours*;
- and David Bowie put out "Fame" and "Young Americans."

Royalty had been redefined, the concert stage now the new temple mount. These artists cemented immortality not through craven attention-grabbing, but by personifying something bigger than themselves.

Meaning and messaging would take an evolutionary leap for the new millennium, as Saturn's 2005–2007 Leo residency launched Twitter, which, at the time, emerged as competition to MySpace and the freshly debuted Facebook. On these platforms, you can literally write what you represent in your bio, so long as it's 160 characters or fewer. For the generation born to this new domain of self-expression, the fundamental question remains the same: What is it you have to say?

The stakes of Saturn's coming tour of Leo (2034–2037) are high, indeed. The cultural institutions of the last century, along with the defining dynasties and world leaders, will be things of the past. A new class of originals must rise to lead us forward. They will have grown up in the mirror-world of social media and will have had to cultivate their own voices to withstand and reshape the algorithm. If you're reading this chapter, it's inevitable that you have a part to play in this revolution.

Here's how to embrace your radical potential. Leo's ruling planet is the sun, which has consistently risen to deliver us life since the beginning of time. In astrology's language of correspondences, you do not merely live under the sun—you *are* the sun. Considering that you have the power to radiate pure solar life upon everything you touch, it's far from selfish to want to know what it is you're about, and what you're projecting. Within your personal orbit, consider who your solar rays influence.

All Saturn Returns involve a relationship reboot, a clearing away of old interpersonal debris. In the case of the Saturn Return in Leo, we are talking about transmissions: what you're reflecting and what's being reflected back to you. As you come into your gifts and confidence, a change in relational frequency will be necessary.

As the archetype of the star, Leo may come off as self-indulgent, but it's a very brave thing to let others see the real you. And it's impossible to come into your gifts in isolation, especially if you want to know where you keep getting in your own way. You need eyes on you, in pursuit not of validation but of accountability. Saturn will force you to consider who in your life really gets you. You may fall out with old confidants who think you're still the person you were at age twenty-three and nothing more. And just as those relationships end, you'll encounter real traveling companions, people you can't wait to collaborate with and learn from.

Who in your life affirms your divine power, and who wants you to silence it so that you don't threaten their insecurities? And, to redirect you from rampant influencer megalomania, I should say: Real friends and mentors, the ones who see you and your highest potential, can and should hold you accountable.

During my Saturn Return (in Capricorn, I should say), I put up a cabaret show. It was liberating, purifying, humiliating, cringe-inducing, worth the risk. I exposed myself in a way I never had before, and learned the hard way what it is to receive unsolicited criticism. Some people I knew felt too comfortable sharing their thoughts. But the input that counted came from my fellow creative peers, offering notes on how my next show could be so much better. I had to learn whose feedback to value.

Beyond others, there's the most sacred relationship of you and your talent. When it comes to Saturn-in-Leo generations, we're talking about true icons, the sort of legends whose names will be remembered eons after they're gone: Charlemagne. Beethoven. Bowie. Mandela. Sylvester. Chadwick Boseman. In all these lives, in all these greatest hits, one can't help but wonder what could—or, shall we say, couldn't—have been. What if Stephen King didn't show up to his desk every day? What if Grace Jones got an office job? What if Georgia O'Keeffe became a dentist? By the push of the planets, they all woke up. So must you—when Saturn returns to Leo. Only the stars know the future impact of your presence, your kindness, your gifts—the way they'll reverberate, the lives they'll change, the subtle shifts they'll have on our collective evolution.

But it's up to you to believe in them now and to take yourself seriously enough to hone your talents. You'll have to stop deflecting compliments, apologizing for taking up space, and canceling yourself for mistakes you haven't even made yet. Treat your life as precious. Address the ways you hide, dissociate, or give power away, all so that you can avoid the true and dazzling solar entity burning through your bathroom mirror.

Over his first Saturn Return in Leo, Austrian bodybuilder Arnold Schwarzenegger debuted the documentary *Pumping Iron*. Decades later, it's still playing in gyms around the world. Generations of young men have not only idolized Schwarzenegger but also taken extreme measures to sculpt their bodies in his exact image. By revealing the grueling commitment to his craft, Schwarzenegger played the role of Saturn, inviting his fandom to push themselves just as hard. Everybody is a star, but very few can keep shining without dedication and consistency.

Consider what it is you need to feel expansive, creative, on solid earth, and not underwater. Regardless of what your creative style looks like—mine is certainly all over the place—make space for it. If you won't start painting unless your house is spotless, go ahead and buy the dish gloves already.

This being a Saturn Return in Leo, a sign whose business is the external, a makeover will be in order. This is a declaration of what you are and your commitment to expressing it.

Think of Saturn-in-Leo Alicia Silverstone, consulting her conveyor-powered wardrobe in *Clueless*, or fellow Saturn-in-Leo Sarah Michelle Gellar, slaying vampires in red leather pants and hoop earrings. If you can design a creative uniform, a means of emerging in the world as your most elevated self, you can signal to Saturn that you believe the hype, that you're worth it.

I can't say when it was that Saturn-in-Leos Ludacris, Marina Abramović, and Stevie Nicks decided that they were going to go in all the way, but once they did, the rest of us followed suit. This is what they do, and you're either obsessed or not, but they're not really stopping to ask for your approval. Over the course of your first Saturn Return in Leo, you'll find your way and not look back.

By the time of his second Saturn Return, Arnold had gone from the world's highest-paid movie star to two-term governor of California. But he departed with low approval ratings and a legacy viewed with ambivalence at best. If you spent your first Saturn Return in Leo finally coming into your solar power, embracing all you have to offer the world, you'll have to consider, this second time around, the risk of burning out.

That's not to say that, come age fifty-five, Spielberg should have quit filmmaking and started knitting, that Nancy Pelosi shouldn't have bothered with the whole "first woman Speaker of the House" thing, or that Iggy Pop should have put on a T-shirt. You're not being asked to disappear, but to consider the service of your talent. Are you leading, teaching, guiding, inspiring? Are you still fulfilling the creative call that is yours to answer? If so, go off, as hard and proud as ever. But if you're stealing the spotlight because you can't bear to break with it, Saturn will force an ugly parting.

In honestly embracing your gifts, you choose a lane and own what is yours and yours alone to do in this world. The temptation has never been greater to take up space, to join in on the noise, to scream for attention. But if you work on your craft, dress the part, and hold yourself accountable, you won't have to fight for the mic. The spotlight will come on, a bellowing voice will announce your name, and you'll know you're ready.

When Saturn Returns to ♍
VIRGO

Key Directives:
Boundaries, self-definition, order, purification

Dates:
August 12, 1919–October 7, 1921
December 19, 1923–April 5, 1924
September 18, 1948–April 2, 1949
May 29, 1949–November 20, 1950
March 7, 1951–August 13, 1951
November 16, 1977–January 4, 1978
July 26, 1978–September 21, 1980
September 2, 2007–October 29, 2009
April 7, 2010–July 21, 2010
October 16, 2036–February 11, 2037
July 8, 2037–September 6, 2039

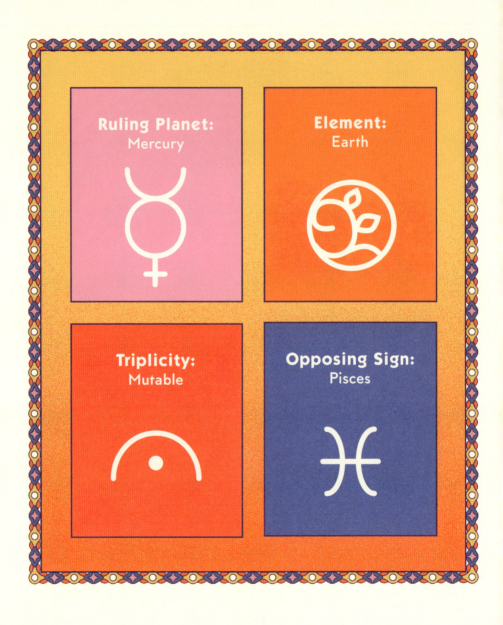

HONOR YOUR BOUNDARIES SO THAT YOU DON'T LOSE YOURSELF.

♍

We have arrived at the midpoint of our journey through the zodiac. The first five signs (Aries through Leo) deepened our knowledge of the self. The signs to come (Libra through Pisces) put that self into contact with the larger world around us. Virgo, then, represents an essential pause, to consider what we are, where we're going, and the protections necessary to move ahead. When Saturn, the planet of boundaries, returns to Virgo, you'll have to set your value so that no one else can sell you away.

Virgo gets its name from the virgin archetype, which, in a Judeo-Christian context, refers to young women who negotiate their worth to secure the ideal matrimonial arrangement and, with it, their future. Of course, for eons before our little monotheistic fad began, *virgin* referred to the vestal virgins, high priestesses whose bodies were considered literal temples to the divine. They were untouchable vessels of the gods whose ritual purity and cultivated ecstasy could open portals and shift realities.

Your body and your personhood are just as sacred. It's why we worship Virgos like Beyoncé or Elizabeth I: They realize their power and elevate themselves above the likes of mere mortals. Their kingdom, their rules. However, the world we live in does not allow for the cultivation of private worth. We all must compromise ourselves in some way, if even just to work to pay rent. Out in the wild, in social survival mode, it's hard to hold on to the divinity afforded to each of us.

It requires tremendous gumption to know who you are and what you're worth, and to not be swayed by others. You know that girl from middle school who always said she "didn't like drama" even though she was always at the center of it? Once said, her words immediately revealed the opposite. My ears perk up when people declare, suddenly and triumphantly, that they don't care what people think. Of course you do. Unfortunately, we live in an environment of social capital, where our worth is determined by others. But if you're to get through your Saturn Return and begin to take yourself seriously, you'll have to start creating boundaries, saying no, and forgiving yourself when you stumble.

The Saturn-in-Virgo Karen Carpenter, born in 1950, had one of the most luminous voices of the twentieth century—a voice which the public hungrily consumed and her family mercilessly peddled. She died shortly after her first Saturn Return in Virgo, enervated and emaciated. We all want to be wanted, and many of us believe that fame will give us the love we were once deprived of. But when people want you, they often want something *from* you, and if you can't set the rules, they'll feast until there's nothing left but the bones.

To be loved greedily and rejected totally are part of the same spectrum. Virgo is linked to the experiences of women and anyone seeking bodily autonomy. When Saturn returns to Virgo, it delivers an experience all women know: backlash. During Saturn's late-'70s tour of Virgo, Stevie Nicks was overrun with hate mail accusing her of witchcraft on account of her all-black wardrobe. For a few years, she gave in, put the coven attire in storage, and wore apricot and seafoam green. Can you imagine? At the same time, disco legend Donna Summer was at the peak of her popularity but was being abused and undervalued by her record executive, denied agency over music she created.

Your sense of self has to be built on something more than the world around you. They may love you today but hate you tomorrow. When Saturn returns to Virgo, you'll likely experience severe polarities as the monoliths of your external reality are shaken and tested. Through the highs and lows, what holds your center, no matter what? I doubt you have the answer to that right now—I certainly don't. But Saturn's harsh instruction will help you discover something immortal and impregnable, something that is yours to hold on to through every cosmic passage.

Of course, there's a mercenary aspect to all this self-preservation. Saturn's tour of Virgo in the late '00s corresponded with a global economic collapse. Saturn-in-Virgo M.I.A. released the hustle-or-die anthem "Paper Planes," and the Joker's cynical worldview—as delivered by Saturn-in-Virgo Heath Ledger—captured our collective imagination via *The Dark Knight*. Our systems of government and finance had failed us, and suddenly it was every person for themselves. Many would bet on themselves in the digital boom to come, making their own lives into personal brands, but as evidenced by the overwhelm of influencers trying to take up space, it can't only be about you.

This is the time to build a life raft for the maelstroms on the horizon, but not to become an island. When Saturn returns to Virgo from 2036–2039, the Alpha generation born to a go-it-your-own-way survivalism will pave new roads toward economic equality. Virgo's recognition of the divine in all of us will lead to new protections for workers and unions. Many will have been raised under digital surveillance, their parents posting pictures of them online since they were infants. They will lead the culture in a comprehensive redefinition of privacy and personal freedoms, setting the rules of engagement in a new world order. As they undergo their Saturn oppositions in Pisces (2023–2026), new laws concerning the mining of our digital data are being passed.

To survive the radioactivity of human relations, you'll need armor. This is where Saturn, a planet of structure, finds a stylish collaborator in Virgo. Consider Saturn-in-Virgo legends Mae West, Aaliyah, and Anna Wintour: They wear fabric like it's chain mail, speak succinctly and firmly, and exude an unimpeachable cool that makes their word unquestionable. What would it mean to retain certain things for yourself, to not overshare? Saturn doesn't want you to live in fearful privacy, but to protect what you share externally, to live by an ethos of less is more.

Saturn enjoys the earthy practicality of Virgo. When setting boundaries, you can be quite literal. Identify who or what makes you feel compromised. Get clear on those stimuli that lead you to betray yourself. Is it a drug? Is it a person? In your career, consider what you offer and how you're compensated. The more specific you get, the less abstract the work ahead.

Great relief awaits you at the end of your first Saturn Return in Virgo, because from here on out, you'll have chosen your lane and set your limits. Those feelings of nebulousness, of being available to everyone, have now been sharpened by your own editorial command of your life: Here's what you do, and here's how you can engage with others without compromising everything.

Those who experience their second and third Saturn Returns in Virgo must concede to the ways they've isolated, hoarded, and become cynical and distrusting. This should be a moment of bright optimism for your sunset era, of wanting to share your gifts with the world and act as mentor to the next generation. To do so, you'll have to let go of some of the safeguards that were adopted over your first Saturn Return. This can be a peaceful release. As you adapt to new modes of communication and collaboration, you get to customize your output and enjoy the silence that comes when you're out of the spotlight.

When Saturn returns to Virgo, the illusory grip over your circumstances will be ripped away; say goodbye to your little manicured life. But as you weather this storm and the next (and the next), as you surrender control, you'll notice what remains. Which values, ethics, and aspects of self make you *you*? By retaining these hard lines, you'll be able to endure any crisis, because you won't have lost yourself along the way.

When Saturn Returns to ♎ LIBRA

Key Directives:
Relationality, collaboration, balance

Dates:
October 7, 1921–December 19, 1923
April 5, 1924–September 13, 1924
November 20, 1950–March 7, 1951
August 13, 1951–October 22, 1953
September 21, 1980–November 29, 1982
May 6, 1983–August 24, 1983
October 29, 2009–April 7, 2010
July 21, 2010–October 5, 2012
September 6, 2039–November 12, 2041
June 22, 2042–July 14, 2042

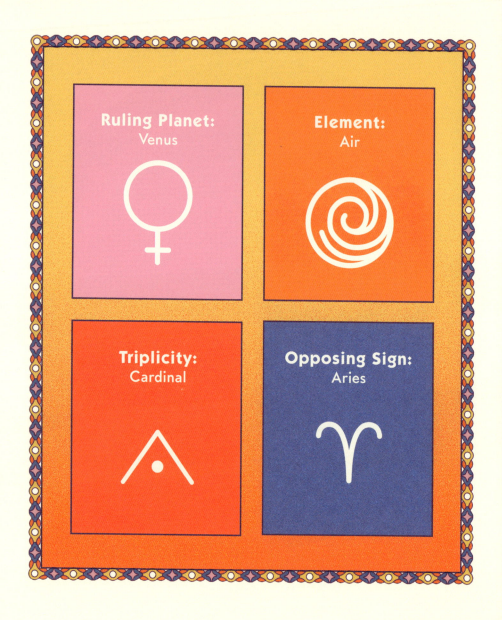

IT'S NOT THEM; IT'S YOU.

♎

We've finally arrived at a sign Saturn favors, where the god of order is exalted. And really, for the governor of the zodiac, what's not to love about Libra, the Versailles of the twelve signs? This is the sign of relationality, social custom, and getting along. Where could that go wrong?

Libra delivers us from the realm of self and into the wide-open world of others: friends, lovers, collaborators, nemeses. We now develop in a relative universe in which we compare ourselves to, and compete with, the people around us. Every person you encounter is a mirror: Every exchange holds the potential for your own clarity or distortion. At Libra's highest vibration, relationships act as vehicles, leading us forward to our shared destinies. But what happens when someone reflects back to us that which we don't like in ourselves? The mirror cracks. When Saturn returns to Libra, it's time to face the other—and forgive what we see of ourselves in them.

Libra is often thought of as the pageant queen of the zodiac, preaching for world peace from her tree in the Garden of Eden. But contrary to the ethos of our individualistic society, the zodiac is very clear: You can only get so far on your own. To make it all the way, to transcend the limits, you're going to have to learn to play with others.

If you grew up with siblings, you learned fast that you're not always the chosen one. Much of the time, it's someone *else* who won the football game, or spilled Hi-C on her prom dress. You're present and essential, and you certainly are entitled to a snack pack, but tonight, it's not about you. Unfortunately, capitalism and social media have instilled in all of us an only child complex.

When Saturn returns to Libra, you'll realize how the projections have run wild, how a need to see yourself—in everything you read and watch, in your elected representatives and sexual partners—has siloed you away from a bigger world, put you on the defensive, kept you from being of a higher service.

A Saturn returning to Libra can, and likely will, involve relationship meltdowns—but the breakup is the symptom. Saturn is interested in the cause: What is it in yourself that you're attracted to, repulsed by, or jealous of *in them*? If we do indeed project ourselves onto everyone we meet, then Saturn will rip out the film and pause the movie. It's time to make some cuts. When Saturn returns to Libra, every encounter will suddenly become a crucible, every interpersonal conflict a lesson. Whatever they did that pissed you off (and vice versa) will likely reveal more about the beholder than the actor. That's what happens when we have to share in the sandbox.

Saturn wants you to think about how you identify, or misidentify, with others. Saturn-in-Libra periods feature movies about people who aren't what they seem, who are hiding under the skin some abject monstrosity: werewolves (*The Howling, An American Werewolf in London*), aliens (*The Thing*), gender deviants (*Victor/Victoria, Tootsie*), androids (*Blade Runner*). When Saturn returned to Libra from 2009 through 2012, President Barack Obama was accused of having forged his American citizenship. The authors of this fiction couldn't forgive a difference of race in their president: If he didn't look like *them*, then he *must* be an infiltrator.

The best movie of Saturn's 2009–2012 Libra return is *Black Swan*, a camp ballerina showdown to the death starring Natalie Portman and Mila Kunis (both experiencing their Saturn Returns in Libra while filming) as two rivals vying for the lead role in *Swan Lake*. Portman starts out the movie shy and repressed, her sexuality and self-expression subsumed by an overbearing mother. When she encounters Kunis's Lily, a libertine who parties hard and lets loose on the stage, Nina sees red. The "black swan" represents everything our innocent ballerina wants to be, but until she can face the power she fears in herself, she'll be trapped with her resentment, unable to let go and join her nemesis as a dancing partner.

Do you see your own blocked potential awakened in someone else? Saturn will force you to face your jealousy and get to the shame or self-abnegation that holds you back from playing in the big leagues. Whatever the conflict is, I can assure you: It's not them; it's you.

How to face your other: First, ensure you have the right friends or therapeutic professionals—not involved in your industry—who can offer you some clear perspective. "It sounds like you're jealous" is something we need our closest confidants to say to our faces once in a while. Second, consider why you feel fixated on your latest nemesis. Does your job, or your social conditioning, inspire a scarcity mentality in you? Perhaps there is something in them that you covet. Consider instead what would happen if you teamed up and took over the matrix together.

Saturn-in-Libra's preferred mirror is the TV screen. It was on the airwaves, during the 1950–1953 era, that the coronation of Queen Elizabeth II was captured and the Academy Awards were first projected to the populace. Come the early-'80s edition, Elizabeth's son Charles would marry Diana Spencer in a televised spectacular watched by over 750 million people worldwide. In 2011, with Saturn back in Libra, Beyoncé revealed her pregnancy onstage at the MTV Video Music Awards. Untouchable idols were brought down to digestible size. You watched them and related: They're just like you.

And yet, the TV screen, like the phone screen, is a boxed-in version of reality, which can be warped to show us what we want to see. Over your first Saturn Return, you'll have to turn the controller off. In the years since Saturn's 2009–2012 Libra edition, it's become common parlance to say you identify as something or with something. Very useful in finding your people, but potentially limiting if it means that you always need to see yourself—in everything you read and watch, in your elected representatives and sexual partners. Some of the big breakthroughs of life, the relationships that change you, can't be made to resemble you. They're supposed to come from something truly other.

By the time of Saturn's next arrival in Libra (2039–2042), those identities that once mattered so much will be discarded as part of a thrilling global exchange. Our understanding of statehood and personhood will undergo radical shifts. Those in their first Saturn Return will be at the cutting edge of a new language, a different means of accepting the other, as previous borders or cultural definers melt away. We will have to cut down the institutions that profit by keeping us in states of narcissistic victimhood.

The pageant queen chirps for world peace, and we laugh at her naivete. But through the work of your first Saturn Return in Libra, you'll have moved a lot of anger, enough to de-weaponize the conflicts you've had with others. You may start to see the world as less hostile, more available for collaboration or coalition. Who knows—if you can cultivate peace in your private orbit, maybe it could reset the entire planet.

Just the same, if your anger doesn't get dealt with, there's the possibility for world-annihilating consequences as you come to your midfifties. You want to end your second Saturn Return feeling open, excited, and pleased to meet strangers (it's good for your health). You don't want to become one of *those* people, blasting fringe AM radio, believing that some troublemaker is coming to steal your silverware. You're too old to be a victim. This rule applies to one's third Saturn Return as well. The next generation won't look or act or sound like you. Be open to them. You might learn something.

"If you can't love yourself, how in the hell you gonna love anybody else?" said RuPaul when Saturn last arrived in Libra. *RuPaul's Drag Race* had only just wrapped its first season, when the titular goddess debuted her immortal axiom. Well? One *should* end any Saturn Return—be it in your late twenties, late fifties, or eighties—with a sense of acceptance and peace. You get the way your inner judgments were wielded over others, how you attracted negative voices to join your own Greek chorus of self-criticism. Now that you see yourself as fine—great, even—you find you don't have as many bones to pick with the rest of the human race. You can finally join, and even change it for the better.

When Saturn Returns to ♏ SCORPIO

Key Directives:
Metamorphosis, rebirth, truth

Dates:
September 13, 1924–December 2, 1926
October 22, 1953–January 12, 1956
May 13, 1956–October 10, 1956
November 29, 1982–May 6, 1983
August 24, 1983–November 16, 1985
October 5, 2012–December 23, 2014
June 14, 2015–September 17, 2015
November 12, 2041–June 22, 2042
July 14, 2042–February 21, 2044
March 26, 2044–November 1, 2044

DEAL WITH THE TRUTH OR DIE IN DENIAL.

No sign inspires fear quite like Scorpio. Even Scorpios are afraid of Scorpios. And perhaps they're not wrong. The eighth sign's purpose is to expose the truth; when a planet or person crosses its gates, a stripping-down is in order. When Saturn returns to Scorpio, it's time to cut the act and accept the hard truths of life.

Scorpio season arrives with the first bitter cold of autumn. The leaves are falling, and the light of summer has faded. Nothing lasts forever. Scorpio moves us through the hard inevitabilities of death and decay. Its evolutionary role is to keep us honest, to ground us in a deeper awareness of life's bracing realities.

In his *Complete Astrology*, Alan Oken likens Pisces to the ocean, Cancer to the rushing river, and Scorpio to the iceberg: We can see but a small shard of ice, but it's enough to change your trajectory forever. A Saturn Return often involves a shock, a wake-up call that rips away the veil. This will likely be the case in Scorpio. A family secret comes spilling out. A routine checkup yields a shocking diagnosis. You learn, all too suddenly, that your partner isn't who they say they are.

When presented with the evidence that our lives are built on a lie, most of us would prefer to go back in the closet and stay there forever. To break us out of stagnation, Saturn in Scorpio has to get dirty, exposing the crumbling monoliths we've put our faith in, breaking our hearts so that we cannot ever be fooled again. Saturn needs you to be here, not living in a fantasy. You can't hide out in your plastic dreamhouse forever, fearing an inevitable ambush. That's not true freedom.

These moments often mark the definitive end of childhood. The point is, it's happened. You're awake. There's no going back. For Scorpio, truth is beauty. It's in those experiences of death or loss or devastation that we can see the guts of a person. Whatever has been hidden—consciously or unconsciously—will force an end to the life you once knew. If you can face it, you can begin the life that Saturn has always intended for you.

Scorpio's pet fixation is taboo, on those markers of abjection or moralism that keep us unquestioning. This is where some deeper, uglier truth is buried, and when Saturn returns to Scorpio, the secret's out. The breaker of hypocrisy, the great terror that levels all towers of good standing, is sex—another favorite of Scorpio's. Saturn-in-Scorpio eras always bring sexual deviancy to the forefront: Oscar Wilde was imprisoned for gross indecency during the fin de siècle edition; the 1953-to-1956 round brought on the explosive carnality of rock 'n' roll, just as Hooverism and the Red Scare sought to contain homosexuals, Jews, and so-called Communist collaborators; 1982 to 1985 saw the devastating outbreak of AIDS, which was met with silence by a homophobic public and presidential administration; and come the 2012-to-2015 return, Laverne Cox would usher in the "Transgender Tipping Point" on the cover of *Time* magazine.

Whatever the taboo is, the discourse around it always exposes our own moralisms, anxieties, and hypocrisies. Saturn will bring your own so-called "bad behaviors" to the forefront. It wants you to break the divide between your public persona and the self you've stashed away in the underworld; to stop being afraid of who you really are, what you've done, what you desire.

By owning the truth, you're signaling to Saturn that you're game, that you're ready to engage in a dialogue and not be a victim of oppression. Over his first Saturn Return in Scorpio, in the mid '50s, Rock Hudson became one of the greatest studs in Hollywood history, the masculine paragon women wanted and men wanted to be. But by the time of his second Saturn Return, in the mid '80s,

Hudson would die trying to hide his AIDS diagnosis and, with it, his decades-long secret life as a gay man. Hudson cleaved to the fictitious role he'd played all his life. But it was the revelation of Hudson's illness that caused a sea change in the cultural response to the AIDS crisis. He helped to break a stigma and save lives, even though he wouldn't be around to see it. Over the same transit, the playwright and activist Larry Kramer debuted his play *The Normal Heart*, an aggressive rebuke to straight society's silence in the face of a deadly epidemic. But in speaking truth to power, he claimed his destiny and showed Saturn—and a world which preferred him dead—that he feared nothing.

The point of this Saturn Return is not to liberate you from *any* ethical framework, but to help you develop an authentic moral compass free from the internalized phantasms of your upbringing. We must unburden you of whatever outdated nonsense your parents, your priest, or your president enforced to keep you herded and compliant. You've been reacting to them for years without knowing it, acting out and replaying the macabre psychosexual operatics you grew up with. If you can face them and own them, you'll no longer be heaving around the weight of your childhood. You'll be free to contemplate what feels right, pleasurable, healthy, and fair—based on reality, not the shadow show in your head.

It will help to not only take ownership over your sexuality but also set it free in all aspects of lived existence. Saturn in Scorpio boasts the greatest-ever roster of sex symbols: Marilyn Monroe, Richard Burton, Marlon Brando, Paul Newman, Billy Idol, and Iman. Of course, *Sex and the City*'s resident libertine Kim Cattrall was born to Saturn in Scorpio. It's not just about sex, it's about truth, about wearing your drive and desire on your sleeve for the world to see. If strapping into leather, slipping into a catsuit, or dying your hair platinum helps bring some part of you to the light, it means you're participating in self-exhumation. You're opening the channels to your interior world so that all your buried gifts and traumas can rise to the surface without judgment.

The first Saturn Return in Scorpio may begin with a shock, but it ends with grounded clarity. So the world isn't perfect. You no longer believe it needs to be. You're out of the closet, no longer walking on eggshells in fear of being outed. You're ready to dance with what Saturn next throws your way.

By the time of your second and certainly third Saturn Returns, you'll have begun to face the precarity of your own mortality. Life is getting shorter. This requires submission to a higher master, the one that will someday claim your life. There is no defense, no amount of money or prestige, that can defer the end. Give in to this transit and you can enjoy the last third of your life as a playful cocreator, here for the ride rather than trying to deny the inevitable.

Your Saturn Return in Scorpio will bring you face-to-face with life's hardest truths. You will cry, and then you will learn to laugh, to marvel at all that is vivid and transient in an unpredictable life. You'll be a great drinking buddy for Saturn and a reliable presence in the lives of others, because when shit gets real, you won't talk in platitudes.

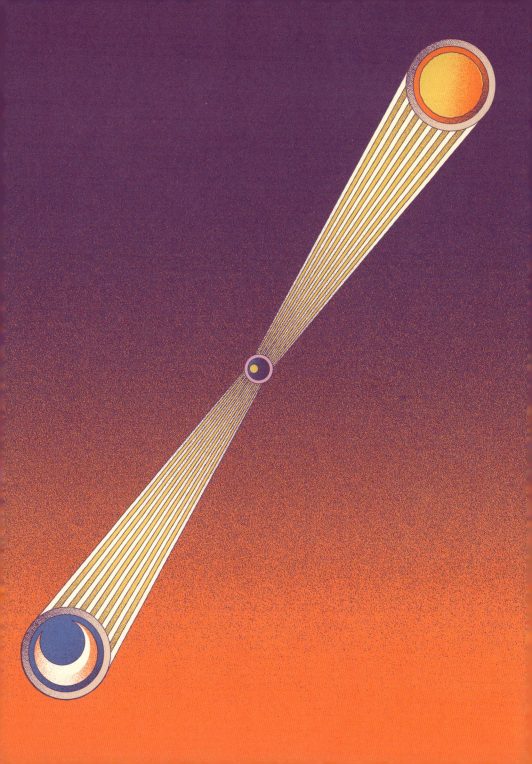

When Saturn Returns to ♐ SAGITTARIUS

Key Directives:
Adventure, spiritual expansion, new horizons

Dates:
December 2, 1926–March 15, 1929
May 4, 1929–November 29, 1929
January 12, 1956–May 13, 1956
October 10, 1956–January 5, 1959
November 16, 1985–February 13, 1988
June 9, 1988–November 11, 1988
December 23, 2014–June 14, 2015
September 17, 2015–December 19, 2017
February 21, 2044–March 26, 2044
November 1, 2044–January 25, 2047
July 12, 2047–October 24, 2047

TIME TO DO WHAT YOU CAME HERE TO DO.

When Saturn returns to Sagittarius, it's time to shoot your shot, make your statement, do what you came here to do. By now you've started to feel it: The event horizon approaches, the tectonic plates are shifting, and the human collective is about to tilt into its next incarnation. We're mere moments away from Saturn's return to its ruling signs, Capricorn and Aquarius, where it initiates a new order. The future is arriving, and you haven't much time before it departs again—with or without you.

Welcome to the sign of the galloping centaur, firing his bow toward the heavens, aiming all his focus toward a singular goal. In the frenzied race to the horizon, there is no looking back, only lunging into the unknown. Saturn Return periods always bring us face-to-face with our mortality, but in the manic language of Sagittarius, the confrontation is a reveille with bugles and trombones, not a funeral dirge. Time to wake up. If the clock really is running out, then what *haven't* you done?

Played correctly, a Saturn Return in Sagittarius *should* be an invitation to ditch your outdated inhibitions and risk it all: to do something massive, something you may regret but that you know is worth it. This could be the moment you become the artist, the hero, the legend you were meant to be—or when you get a dolphin tattoo on your backside. Even if it ends in humiliation, no one will say that you didn't live your life to the fullest.

You know how I, a Sagittarius rising, rode the currents of Saturn's 2014 to 2017 centaur epic? While working as a magazine editor, I started moonlighting as a go-go dancer. In the wee hours of the workweek, you could find me stripping for cash, rent money, and eternal glory. Writing this book in the blissful dotage of my thirties, would I dare do any of these things now? Certainly not for dollar bills. Do I look back and grin—at my naivete, my *chutzpah*, my desire to experience everything? Absolutely.

There are certain experiences you must have now—in this liminal crossing, when you've got nothing to lose—that simply won't be possible once you're more established. Saturn-in-Sagittarius eras are boom periods for risk-taking on the cultural stage, inspiring creators from all generations, no matter their Saturn placement. Over the 1985-to-1988 tour:

- Saturn-in-Sagittarius Tim Burton crafted his satirical ghoul masterpiece, *Beetlejuice*;
- *The Simpsons* launched as an experimental animated short on *The Tracey Ullman Show*;
- Robert Zemeckis somehow convinced Disney to let him make *Who Framed Roger Rabbit?*;
- Jim Henson and David Bowie gave us *Labyrinth*, a theatrical bomb that became a cult classic;
- and Andrew Lloyd Weber launched his gaudy camp spectacular *The Phantom of the Opera*, which would become Broadway's longest-running show.

During the 2014 to 2017 Sagittarius era, Rihanna and Beyoncé took artistic left turns with *Anti* and *Lemonade*, respectively, and Warner Brothers took a chance on a female-centered superhero movie with *Wonder Woman*.

All legendary now but enormous risks back then, many of which shouldn't have worked. So what are you afraid of doing, or saying, or putting out? What if it isn't highbrow or polished enough? What if it goes down in flames? The time will come for you to make measured choices, to choose your moment—but right now it's the opposite.

Saturn is the god of time, and, unfortunately, it does run out. A universal Saturn Return experience is that of the ten-year (and forty-year) high school reunion, when we go back and see how everyone has—or, more crushingly, has not—changed since the old days. Here, you'll encounter the ones who never quite got out, never went for their dreams, never left the family mattress business, never did bad acid in Montreal. Saturn will force you out of complacency so that you do not end up like one of these people.

There's a reason Luke Skywalker's farm burns down just when he's considering the whole Jedi-initiation thing. There must be no going back. Certain crises will be introduced to throw you into the fire. It may be a divorce that pushes you out of the suburbs and into an ashram, or a financial meltdown that takes away your art studio, forcing you to begin again with a glue stick and old magazines. Regardless, it's now or never.

But that doesn't mean you should toss yourself around. Saturn has a clear design for you, a trajectory in mind. These choices matter. In the sign of daring, the planet of restraint doesn't want you leaping onto the next boat with no idea where you're going. Though you're encouraged to ditch caution, you should be wary of the longing for the solution to all life's problems just over this cliff, and then over the next. Saturn wants you to change your life but not to lose yourself along the way.

If you're aimless, alone, without community or a sense of purpose, there is no cause that can restore you to wholeness. Sagittarius is the sign of the seeker, the one who wanders, studies, and engages on the quest for meaning. This is not a voyage that can be expedited. If you think you've found it—the belief, the movement, the charismatic religious leader who just needs access to your bank's routing number—then you're in trouble. There is indeed an adventure that awaits only you, but it can't be an escape. A Saturn Return in Sagittarius is all about false stars, failed experiments, and outrageous risks. Let yourself play around, and be wary of anything that feels like a divine answer to all your problems.

By launching your adventure without some real ethos girding it, you may end up another brave warrior in a holy war, a false hero puffing up empty machismo. Saturn's 2014 to 2017 tour of Sagittarius recruited militant extremists in Iraq, Syria, Myanmar, and the United States. Lost and lonely young men became Proud Boys, marching with torches at "Unite the Right" rallies. Conversely, the mid-'80s edition saw the formation of ACT UP, or the AIDS Coalition to Unleash Power, which saved countless lives through focused and strategic counteroffensive against the US government and pharmaceutical industries. ACT UP channeled the rage and grief of its broad coalition toward real and tangible goals, meant to prevent more needless death. It was grounded in something real.

Saturn wants to keep you on Earth. Fly too close to the sun, and you may go down in flames. I've worked with clients who came to sobriety over their Saturn Return in Sagittarius, who went too far and had to find their threshold the hard way. Indeed, the journey of learning one's limits is as great and psychedelic a voyage as any, and Saturn will be there when you crash-land, waiting with a hose, ready to help you back up again.

Saturn is investing in you, and would be wholly disappointed if you were to finally launch, only to congeal back into fear and laziness after a few failures. To ensure that you're still riding high come your second return / fortieth high school reunion, Saturn will condition you for long-distance running. My Sagittarius friend Emily always says: If it's urgent, it's not spiritual. So you'll learn to question all-or-nothing imperatives. Consider what you need to make your best and most embodied life sustainable. What is the part-time gig that ensures the health of your artistic life? What do you need to not burn out? It took guts for you to leap out of your old life; it will take mastery to keep your new one running.

The Sagittarians in my life have no fear of asking questions, even if it means they'll come off as ignorant. They're down to explore any spiritual path or social movement, so long as there's no binding contract. This freedom ensures a long, malleable, adaptive life. Be like the supreme Saturn in Sagittarius, Madonna: Let yourself go through phases. This first Saturn Return will be the most intense experimental era of your life so far. But what comes after is an ongoing dance with ideas and beliefs, the changing steps of which delight you rather than cause you to trip on the floor.

The opposite path is one of entrenchment, the kind that defined Saturn's 2016 election freak show in Sagittarius. Over your first Saturn Return, you may see yourself as up and coming, an underdog, a rebel. Come your second and third round, you may find it seductive to pick a side or, worse, to "take a stand," so as to feel brave and relevant once more. You're missing the point. When Saturn returns a second time to Sagittarius, you could act as a wise master, a voice of perspective cultivating the wisdom of many personal eras, lessons, and failures. You will be free to collaborate with the coming generations, to encourage your peers and your successors to try something new.

You're certain to court failure when you ditch the old digs. Risk does not always yield immediate reward. Saturn will coach you through all the mistakes you inevitably make, but the point is, at least you made them. You've departed the realm of *ifs*. No matter what comes next, there's no looking back.

When Saturn Returns to ♑ CAPRICORN

Key Directives:
Governance, authority, sustainability, survival

Dates:
March 15, 1929–May 4, 1929
November 29, 1929–February 23, 1932
August 13, 1932–November 19, 1932
January 5, 1959–January 3, 1962
February 13, 1988–June 9, 1988
November 11, 1988–February 6, 1991
December 19, 2017–March 21, 2020
July 1, 2020–December 16, 2020
January 25, 2047–July 12, 2047
October 24, 2047–January 22, 2050

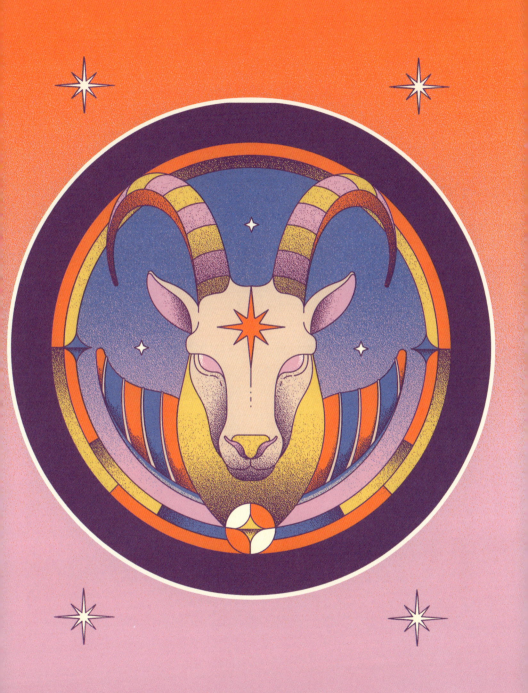

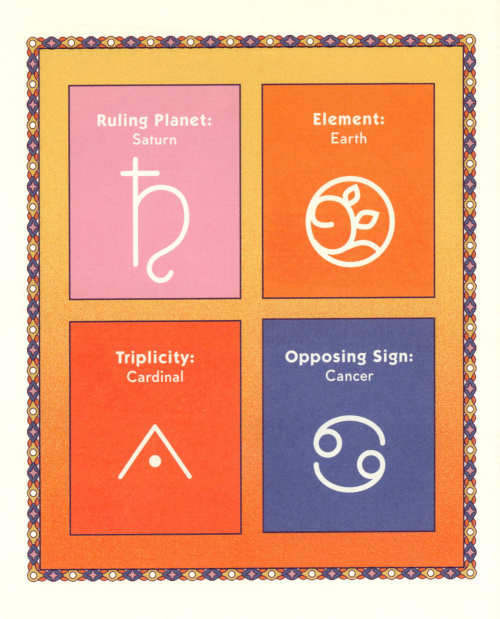

TAKE RESPONSIBILITY FOR YOUR POWER.

♑

Daddy's home. Every planet has a sign (or two) over which it rules, and after a long voyage through the zodiac, Saturn has finally returned to its roost. When Saturn returns to Capricorn, the grand master of the solar system can roll up his sleeves and get to work. Now that the boss is back at the factory, he expects only the best. When Saturn returns to Capricorn, the stakes are nothing less than absolute power—and you're going to have to fight for your stake in the new world order. It is time to take your place and claim what's yours.

Capricorn is the first sign of the winter season, when the primary concern is paying for the heat and keeping the lights on. Unless you want to live like the Bucket family from *Willy Wonka and the Chocolate Factory*—with all four grandparents piled onto one mattress—*someone's* going to have to step up and take responsibility. With necessity comes drive, and with drive emerges ambition, and so Capricorn delivers us the powerhouses, dominators, and masters destined to rule over the rest of us, in either kindness or cruelty. Which will you be?

Remember, Saturn's best-known mythological avatar is Kronos, the original father of the gods who literally devoured his offspring to prevent their ascension to his throne (HBO's *Succession*, a boardroom reimagining of Olympian intergenerational squabbling, was one of the smash debuts of Saturn's 2017–2020 tour in Capricorn). Traditionally, Saturn is thought to represent the father in one's natal chart: that domineering, authoritative presence who may empower or cripple us. All things being equal, for many of us, that role is instead played, with gusto, by our mothers. One way or another, everyone has to face their creator.

As Kronos inevitably fell to his children, Saturn-in-Capricorn regimes always signal the toppling of an old era: We're talking the Great Depression, the demolition of the Berlin Wall, the outbreak of COVID. When the 2020 pandemic tore through our systems of governance and even social interaction, it was like Dad had gone out to buy smokes and never come back. No one was in charge. In the throes of my Saturn Return in Capricorn, I felt like I'd been left behind, like I wasn't ready to take care of myself now that the babysitter was dead. Those feelings would have a deeper origin.

We learn about power, or powerlessness, from our parents, the original authority figures in our lives. And so a Saturn Return in Capricorn will deal with our progenitors and the role they've played in shaping us. I've read a lot of Saturn-in-Capricorn clients who come off as meek or twee in fear of resembling their greedy, grotesque fathers. Saturn needs you to take up a position of leadership, to wield power fairly and justly, so that come 2047, the generation born to this transit won't inherit an even bigger mess. For you to become parent to the world, you have to heal your inner kid.

"Aren't you too old to be blaming it all on your parents?" asks a voice in your head, which sounds remarkably like your parents'. Probably. But if you've been engaging with the damages of the past via passive aggression and denial, it's just perpetuating the problem. We need to blast this case open and get it over with. Saturn loves accounting, so you might as well just put it all on the table, down to your disastrous Bar Mitzvah party. Once it's hashed out, you really may be able to move on, let your parents enjoy their golden years in Boca Raton, and embrace the possibility of your own limitless future.

Remember that Capricorn and Cancer—representing the father and the mother archetypes, respectively—are at a polarity on the wheel of the zodiac. There's a direct dialogue between how we were fed (Cancer) and how we will one day bring home the bacon (Capricorn). So yes, this is going to be one of *those* Saturn Returns, involving hours of therapy, endless screaming matches with your cousin Ruth, dusty photo albums, ancient family secrets, Al-Anon qualifications, and bad poetry about how your father missed your fourth-grade talent show performance. You have to exhume it all, get it out and laugh at it, so that it's no longer ruling your life.

You know what happened during Saturn's last blowout in Capricorn, amid the 2020 global pandemic and economic collapse? A lot of late-twentysomethings moved back in with their parents. The world was melting down, and they had no choice but to help Ma and Pa wash the dishes and keep each other company. And once the dust settled and they could get jobs again, they were able to move out and maybe move on with some new fathoming of their forebears: the rebellion over, the war conceded.

I'm not saying every Saturn Return in Capricorn should end with a sentimental embrace, as Mother knits by the fire and Papa lights the Christmas tree. My Saturn Return in Capricorn was less an episode of *Family Matters* and more of a visit to the Bates Motel. Revelations from the past damaged some familial relationships beyond repair, liberated others, and threw me out of the dollhouse forever. Childhood, and its delusive comforts, had been ripped away, and now I was an adult, really awake for the first time, free to walk my destiny. It wasn't easy, but no birth is.

Many of us go through our twenties waiting for approval to begin our lives. By the end of a Saturn Return in Capricorn, you won't feel as though you're waiting in the cosmic breadline, but that you're the architect of your own fate. You've faced your fears around owning power and even abusing it. Over this period in Capricorn, Saturn selects the new leaders of the age. I'd prefer it if you—in all your introspection, integration, and self-awareness—were my overlord rather than some blowhard who inherited

Daddy's hedge fund and a lack of compassion. The guard has changed, and you've been promoted. Be nice to your underlings because they'll be coming up next.

And what happens when you have embraced the role of father, boss, master, and magnate, when you've made it to your midfifties or mideighties? Classically, the bulk of the #MeToo revelations, concerning powerful men in Hollywood and government, went down during Saturn's 2017–2020 Capricorn era. A lot of men got too complacent and thought they could get away with murder. And because of how unfairly power had been allocated, justice had to be delivered outside of the system, often without due process, to correct grave imbalances. If you do pass the trials of your first Saturn Return and embrace your right to rule, remember that you will inevitably be replaced—whether peacefully or forcefully is up to you. You have the chance to create a new system, a new hierarchy, a sphere of influence in your life. Treat all with respect, embrace mentorship, or else Saturn will be too happy to deliver your comeuppance.

In 2047, the next Saturn-in-Capricorn generation born will meet their adulthood. They will be the ones to put us in old-age homes (or turn us into dog food) and call the shots for the next era of life on Earth. It would *help* if we didn't load them up with our baggage, our history, our intergenerational *mishegoss*. It may prove critical if we, now acting as the gods of the old world, give them something to aspire to and not just another relic to burn down. Your childhood is over. It's time to take responsibility for the future.

When Saturn Returns to
AQUARIUS

Key Directives:
Idealism, revolution, future-thinking, the big picture

Dates:
February 23, 1932–August 13, 1932
November 19, 1932–February 14, 1935
January 3, 1962–March 23, 1964
September 16, 1964–December 15, 1964
February 6, 1991–May 20, 1993
June 29, 1993–January 28, 1994
March 21, 2020–July 1, 2020
December 16, 2020–March 7, 2023
January 22, 2050–April 18, 2052
August 10, 2052–January 12, 2053

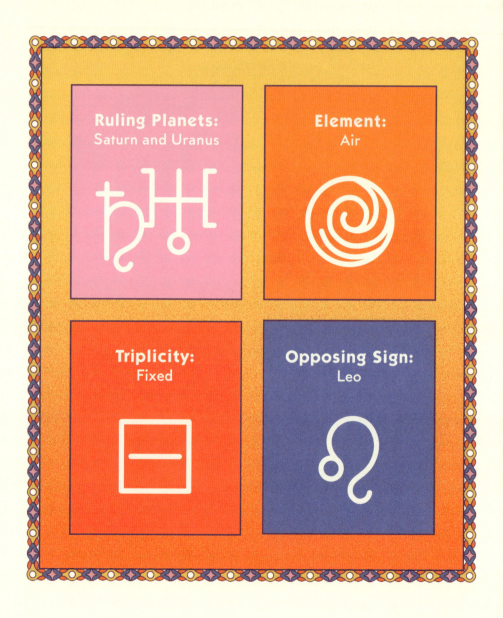

DON'T BRING YOUR BULLSHIT INTO THE NEW WORLD ORDER.

We're nearing the end of the zodiac, a time when consciousness shifts from personal to collective, and we are called to think big about the shape of our shared reality. When Saturn returns to Capricorn, it breaks down the decaying monoliths of our fathers' rule. But in Aquarius, the sign of youth and technology, it's time to create something new. Like any fluid child of the future, Aquarius has *two* rulers: Saturn, planet of order, and Uranus, planet of change. The battle between generations can be enlivening, exhausting, and, occasionally, productive . . . so long as we have our priorities straight. When Saturn returns to Aquarius, you'll either take your place in the future or get caught reenacting the violations of the past.

Aquarius can be thought of as the punk, the alien, the riot grrrl of the zodiac. In Capricorn, Saturn tore down the Berlin Wall and detonated the stock market. Now what? It's out with the old, and time for the revolution. Saturn-in-Aquarius eras signal new technologies (the personal computer, the World Wide Web, and even that gooey liquid metal from *Terminator 2*) and social movements (including the 1963 March on Washington, Rachel Carson launching the environmental movement with her 1962 book, *Silent Spring*, and the Black Lives Matter protests of 2020).

If you arrived on this planet during one of these epochal meltdowns in the fall of late capitalism, you may naturally see yourself as part of the new guard, inherently different from your predecessors and peers, the ones who never questioned the matrix we're all in. Unfortunately, an outsider identity is just as much a cover as any other.

Saturn-in-Aquarius periods always yield quantum leaps in technology, which usually involve some new vanguard of geniuses getting too rich, too fast, without any consequences. As Jeff Bezos rode a rocket into space to celebrate his second Saturn Return in Aquarius, so did years of abuse and unregulated shenanigans in Silicon Valley come to light. This new class of tech billionaires were once clever kids given the reins to reshape our reality, believing themselves mavericks and outcasts even as they became overlords. Under the proviso that they were changing the world for the better, they didn't need to be held accountable. And now many of them have more power than Alexander the Great.

For you to be of the highest service to Saturn's plan, you'll want to keep a clear eye on your own bullshit. Saturn has a specific and essential part for you to play in the future, so if you haven't processed your feelings toward dear old Papa, you'll come off as one of those riotous upstarts, going through what Dionne describes in *Clueless* as a "postadolescent idealistic phase." Or you may get high on power, believing yourself to be a cowboy like the tech bros who now own our private data, all while telling yourself that you're a part of the revolution. No matter how fast the world is changing, you must develop a steady and consistent means of personal accountability.

Saturn's 1962–1964 Aquarius era debuted the X-Men, a band of superpowered mutants, hated and feared by the rest of the human populace. Arriving just as Martin Luther King Jr. and Malcolm X would preach differing philosophies in the Civil Rights revolution, the mutants of the fictional X-Universe would spend decades in constant battle over their place as *Homo superior*. Some wanted to build peace with humanity, some to dominate, some to assimilate. The ostensible villain of the book, Magneto, survives the Holocaust only to rise as a mutant supremacist. Over the years, as the character deals with his past, his mission becomes more holistic. He is still a powerhouse, but he acts more as a protector than an extremist. Let's hope that over time the fleece vest–wearing tech bros see similar errors in their ways, adjusting their course to bring progress into the future rather than repeating past cycles.

In these eras of social upheaval, we zoom out to consider the human race at large, but that doesn't mean we should lose ourselves in the story. During Saturn's recent tour in Aquarius, I had clients apologize to me for even bringing up their personal issues during readings—there were bigger things happening globally. You're not selfish for needing to take space, to go inward and heal yourself, just because the world is on fire. Magneto starts out as a megalomaniac, blind to his own rage. He evolves into a heroic force only through awareness of his own limits. If something is setting you off, you should pull back and deal with it so you can come back to the picket line, secure in yourself to help others.

With the revolution comes the backlash, as Saturn-in-Aquarius periods always spell out culture wars—a bummer for everyone involved (a feature of the early-'90s edition were punishingly lame Senate hearings about the moral danger of video games). It's not that the debates over race, gender, environmental responsibility, and nuclear capability are not important; it's just that everyone tends to take themselves very seriously.

Beware the lure of prescribed moral standards, because if your parents, your friends, and this week's vaguely disgraced celebrity don't pass the test, then guess who's next? Saturn wants you to contribute your gifts to the awakening of the One, the singular mind of a connected planet. Your path will involve messiness, humiliation, and, hopefully, personal accountability—even grace. The world may lose an essential voice if you've preemptively canceled yourself. Over this Saturn Return, you have the opportunity to develop your own ethos, one that allows for subtlety and creativity. That way, no one has to lose their heads for the sake of perfection.

Over your first Saturn Return in Aquarius, you'll reconcile your outsider identity so that you may depersonalize your own nonsense and be of use to a larger conversation. If you're waiting for the world to be pure, for capitalism to be less corrupt, for your chosen industry to be lovely, for your ideals to be respected, you may miss your chance to board the *Starship Enterprise*. The legends of Saturn in Aquarius know how to sneak punk rock, avant-garde philosophies into the language of the masses: Think RuPaul, Grant Morrison, Quentin Tarantino, Yoko Ono, Salvador Dalí, and Cardi B. You have to learn how to laugh with the times.

The Aquarian chapter of a Saturn revolution will indeed always be revolutionary. The humility promised this time around comes from exposure to ideas and people beyond your small frame of reference. At first, you may feel you need to prove that you're on the right side or that you think a certain way. But as you come to accept your own complicated nature and perceive those around you in subtle layers, you'll be able to address the crises life brings without jumping to moral extremes.

Over your second round, you may find yourself on the opposite side of the culture wars. During his second Saturn Return in Aquarius, RuPaul, now the monarch of an unprecedented, globally adored drag empire, came under fire. The queer and trans communities wanted *Drag Race*, in its language and casting, to better represent them. Inevitably, RuPaul gave in. Let the kids do it their way, and bring their innovations to his dollhouse. Better that than to miss a chance at compromise and the flexibility to change with the times.

Come your midfifties and eighties, you'll really need to inspect the values you're so dearly defending. That's not to say that all youth movements are right—in fact, they could definitely do with your wisdom and perspective, as a mentor and teacher. But if you're cleaving desperately to your old stories of rebellion, you're going to be first in line for the guillotine. How have you been seduced by power and riches? How are you still indulging some fantasy of renegade heroism while acting like a dominator? What if you could make your matrix into a space of dialogue, play, and open exchange?

Saturn will return to Aquarius in 2050, by which time life as we know it may be entirely determined by algorithms and efficiency, a *Soylent Green* "utopia" with no room for human messiness. What will inevitably endure and emerge as *truly* revolutionary will be ambiguity, subtlety, and raw emotion. If you can learn to bring your pain and perspective into the glaringly bright future and take responsibility for what's yours, we may have a chance at a happy ending, with no need for the machines to save us.

When Saturn Returns to ♓ PISCES

Key Directives:
Synthesis, empathy, compassion, surrender

Dates:
February 14, 1935–April 24, 1937
October 17, 1937–January 14, 1938
March 23, 1964–September 16, 1964
December 15, 1964–March 3, 1967
May 20, 1993–June 29, 1993
January 28, 1994–April 6, 1996
March 7, 2023–May 24, 2025
August 31, 2025–February 13, 2026
April 18, 2052–August 10, 2052
January 12, 2053–March 24, 2055

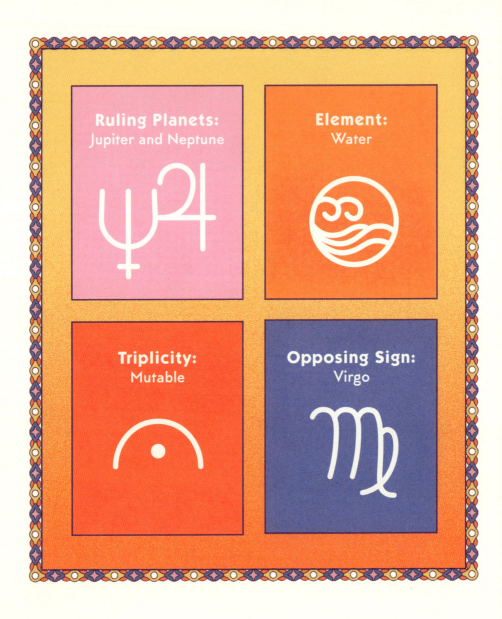

DROP YOUR DELUSIONS OF GRANDEUR AND GET ON WITH YOUR LIFE.

♓

The zodiac is coming to an end, and with it, the world we have known. Who will come to save us? Who will die for our sins so that we may live on? The Age of Pisces began with the crucifixion of Jesus Christ, making this the sign of the martyr, delivering us into the next epoch. You're advised *not* to audition for the role. When Saturn returns to Pisces, you'll have to drop your messianic delusions of grandeur, peel yourself off the cross, and get on with your life.

Pisces commands the ocean of human consciousness, where all the detritus of the zodiac washes up. Here, we are connected to everything, to *all* the power and pain. During Saturn-in-Pisces eras, forces beyond human conception rise, with the potential to liberate or annihilate us. Previous editions have included the French Revolution, the global fever known as Beatlemania, the advent of immersive video games and artificial intelligence, and, as of this writing, the consequences of the opioid epidemic (which has claimed over five hundred thousand American lives so far).

Is it any wonder, then, that during Saturn-in-Pisces eras we see the departure of luminaries thought to be too pure for this world? Kurt Cobain left us during his first Saturn Return in Pisces, and Sinead O'Connor during her second. There is a romantic—and delusive—allure to mythologizing these martyrs.

We all seek escape, one way or another, and in these eras, the Neptunian abyss of drugs, digital worlds, and political turmoil seems ready to swallow us whole. Saturn, however, wants you here: present and active, part of the solution, and ready to cross the Nile. It's time to wake up, get sober, and play a useful part.

The mid-'60s era brought us *Mary Poppins* and *Star Trek*, both of which espouse service over tragic heroism. Poppins has indeed arrived as something of a psychedelic shaman for the Banks family, but in reality, she's just going to work. As for the crew of the *Enterprise*, everyone has their role and seeks to fulfill it with the highest integrity. You likely have a vocation that is yours and only yours to fulfill. Saturn wants you to do it, not because you're the second coming, but because it's your job.

When Saturn returns to Pisces, it yields many chosen ones, destined to uphold a great legacy. But to do that, they need longevity, and that requires showing up. Notable Saturn in Pisces include:

- Queen Victoria, who spent sixty-three years on the throne
- Former bad boy Robert Downey Jr., who got sober and became the iron pillar of the multi-billion-dollar Marvel Cinematic Universe
- Sarah Jessica Parker, the steward of the immortal institution known as *Sex and the City*
- Jane Fonda, still at the front of the picket lines sixty years later

Parker is in her second Saturn Return during 2024, going strong with *Sex and the City*'s sequel series *And Just Like That*. In order to play Carrie, a character who inspires the fascination and ire of millions, Parker doesn't read any reviews or clippings. That's her way of taking care of herself. For anyone to not only step into their power but also maintain it, they have to be aware of their sensitivities, of what they need to stay solid along the way.

Over your first Saturn Return, you'll accept these vulnerable parts within you. Pisces is traditionally known as the sign of self-sabotage; it reveals to us where we lack protection not only from the outside world but from ourselves. Those larger forces that threaten us are, unfortunately, within us. Downey Jr. had to get sober before he could fully embrace his destiny. In setting the terms for your continuous health and happiness, you'll be forced to face your own worst behaviors.

In the terminology of twelve-step recovery, what are your shortcomings? Consider those stimuli that cause you to lose yourself. What are your insobrieties: alcohol, codependency, gambling? Pisces is the sign of the victim, and as you near the end of your twenties, you won't be able to play that card much longer. Where do you need help? Which behaviors prove to always end in self-sabotage? Once you get clarity on what you can't manage, you can find help and consistent ways to stay honest.

We need some protection to endure in the interconnected human ocean. When Saturn returns to Pisces, we learn how to build boundaries with which to protect ourselves, hard lines to keep us from being assimilated. It's not about moral purity or escaping the mess altogether. Indeed, in *The Matrix*, Saturn-in-Pisces Keanu Reeves awakens from his drip-drip slumber, comes to realize that his reality was a lie, and then learns how to master the simulation; to play with it, to reenter the Matrix without losing himself.

It's terrifying to realize that it's all been a lie, a dream, a fairy tale, and that the world is much crueler than we could have imagined. We will all experience loss, devastation, and, possibly, the apocalypse. So how do you want to deal? When Saturn returns to Pisces, you have the chance to really grieve what's been lost by developing the creative, spiritual, and therapeutic practices needed to heal. Maybe it's painting with watercolors, or praying to your ancestors, or taking Zumba classes. It's whatever helps.

The alternative, as previously mentioned, is to take your grief onto the world stage, playing victim for all to see. Be careful not to make it, whatever *it* is—world wars, global pandemics, or public tragedies—about you. You need to get clear on what is your baggage, your pain, and your story, and what isn't. That's not to say that you should cut yourself off from compassion. Quite the opposite. It's just that if you start to play hero, savior, or martyr, you'll likely forget who you are underneath the role.

Over your first Saturn Return in Pisces, you'll learn to view your life from a place of ambivalence. You are indeed the most important person in the world, and you're a mere drop in the ocean. By tending to your issues, you keep your head above water rather than let yourself be consumed by doom or delusory salvation. You take your small part in facing the great tidal changes coming to our world, without being overpowered. You prove to Saturn that you're here to stay.

Come your second Saturn Return in Pisces, you're no longer at the behest of the storms, but at their command. You may be the face of the franchise, the leader of the movement, the captain of the *Enterprise*. You have the power to influence people. What does that responsibility entail? Focus on your role and delegate the rest. This is a time to confront delusions of grandeur. You're not the world, nor will you be on it forever. But what you build, or embody, can outlive you. Tend to it with humility.

There's no greater disappointment than false deliverance. Revolutions rarely fulfill their promises. Drugs lift us to the heavens, then bring us crashing down. And technology has proved to be as fallible and biased as its creators. Many lose their lives under the lure of these overwhelming forces, often not knowing any better. Pisces is the sign of the two fish, one that swims with the current and the other that pushes upstream. Come 2052, a new generation, born to technological innovations and environmental catastrophes we can't imagine, will have its own awakening. They will look upon generations of forebears as either pigs led to the slaughter, or voices of reason. If you can find a way to not get swept up in the current, to keep your wits about you, you may play a part in shaping the world to come. Only you know what you need to stay afloat.

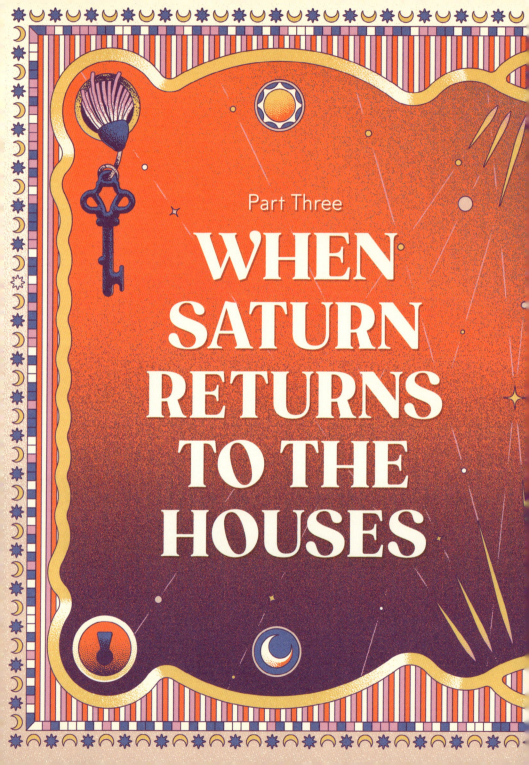

Part Three

WHEN SATURN RETURNS TO THE HOUSES

THE HOUSES

Knowledge of one's sign placement can provide sustenance but not much specificity. It's like eating with your hands. But by picking up a fork, pointing it at the next target, and cutting it to size, you go from frenzied consumer to conscious diner. The houses allow you to focus your gaze, to grasp every chapter of your chart, to view the whole as the sum of its parts.

If you can get a handle on the basic angles of your chart, you will know where the action is going down, for you, at any moment in your life. The meaning of the houses is set for everyone, which is to say, the time of day may change, but the numbers on the clock remain the same. Based on your birth time, we understand where the signs and planets fall on your houses. From there, we can interpret.

It all begins with the ascendant, which is like the big ticker on a roulette wheel. It occupies the nine o'clock position of your chart. The sign that it falls on will be your *rising sign*, and will occupy the first house of your chart. Now we're onto something. I was born with Sagittarius rising, which means that the sign Sagittarius can be found at the western end of my chart, kicking off the first house. Its opposite sign, Gemini, will be at the east, launching the seventh house. Because I was born with this placement, it's set forever. To see what's going on with me now, any current movement of the planets would be explored from the perspective of my chart setup.

You're going to kill me, but there's one more thing. Even though it's all constructed like a clock, the houses, signs, and planets move *counterclockwise*. So, as you start with the ascendant, you're following the planets down through the first six houses of the self and up into the public houses. The rising sign is the start and end of the chart, the closing of one story and opening of another. This sets the themes of the Edda we embark on. When I look at a client's chart, I begin with the rising sign for comprehension of the aesthetic and direction of the chart. Then I consider the placement of the planets in the context of the houses. Interestingly enough, the signs offer us shape and style but should be added last in the recipe.

Let's say you were born in early July 1990, which means you're of the Saturn-in-Capricorn generation. But once I have your birth time and see that Libra is your rising sign, marking the start of your chart, I can see that Saturn is in your fourth house of home, roots, and family. And look! Saturn is in opposition with your sun in Cancer, in your tenth house of career and ambition. Now we have a lot to work with.

We will explore the meanings of each house in the chapters to come. But before progressing, we should get into the weeds about how the chart is constructed. Stick with me here . . .

I mentioned that the chart functions like a clock, and indeed, it is meant to align with the revolution of the sun on the day you were born. Note that one revolution covers twenty-four hours, not twelve, and we move "backward" through night and then into day as we travel counterclockwise. The *ascendant*, at the western position, corresponds with dawn. It represents the death and rebirth of the chart, the transition from night to day. The *midheaven*, or MC, is the noon point, at the summit of your chart, kicking off your tenth house of public visibility and career achievement. At this point in the day, you're thriving at the office, as it were. We come to the *descendant* at dusk, launching the seventh house of others. This is sunset, when you return home to your sweetheart or meet the girls for drinks after work. Finally, the *Imum Coeli*, or IC, hits at midnight, when we're tucked in bed at home. It is located at the base of your chart, at the fourth house of home, roots, and conditioning.

You are not expected to memorize the twelve houses of your chart anytime soon. But it's worth grasping the general meaning of these four angles. The positioning of natal and transiting planets around these key lines always indicates core narratives and lessons coming to a head.

- West deals with the dawning of the self.
- North brings you to public visibility.
- East is the mess hall of friends and lovers.
- South is the root or base, where we grow up and get nourished.

Based on the dawn-to-dusk makeup of the chart, we regard the first six houses as the night half of the chart—these houses deal more with the self and its fundamental motivations. Houses seven through twelve thrust us into day, and themes of relationships and public life.

As with the signs, you're better off considering the houses in relation to one another. We can view Leo in opposition to Aquarius, as two halves of a whole. Similarly, the fifth and eleventh houses should be seen in dialogue. Consider the role of each house in the sequence of the entire chart. Rather than try to memorize each one, try to see them as part of one continuous story.

Remember that the planets are constantly moving through all the signs and interacting with one another in endless combinations. If you were born with more planets in one part of your chart than in another, it doesn't mean that you're deficient, just that this may be the lens through which we focus our exploration.

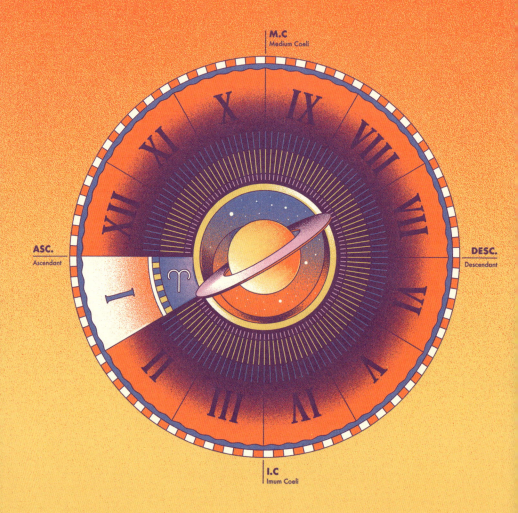

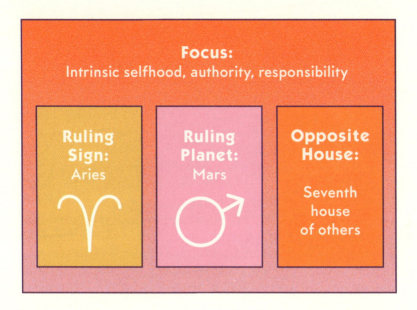

If we are to look at the zodiac as an egg, then the ascendant represents the hatching point. *Hello, world, here I am.* In the twelve-part saga of your cosmic evolution, the first house marks the opening credits, establishing the settings and intrinsic elements of selfhood. What does it mean, then, if one of the first archetypes we encounter, upon arriving here, is stern, serious Saturn? If you were born with Saturn in the first house, then what happens when, after a twenty-eight-year tour through our chart, Saturn finally comes back to ground zero, square one, the scene of the crime? When Saturn returns to the first house, you will parent yourself through your own rebirth.

I liken the first house to day one on planet Earth, when we wake up in the hospital room, take a look at our circumstances, and realize that *this* is it. We can't request a refund. House one deals with the fundamentals. When looking at this house, we consider the drives and attributes that define you.

Because the ascendant is the sign that was rising over the eastern horizon—dawn—the moment you were born, we can think of any planets in the first house as immediate presences in your life. They were right there, looking down on you, from the second you got here. This can indicate that you are destined to embody that planet: So if you were born with Saturn in your first house, you may act as a force of authority or responsibility in your family and close relationships.

When Saturn returns to its place in the first house, it will challenge you to fully step into its function. Saturn is the planet of shape, form, order, and responsibility. Its presence in the first house indicates that you are meant to take total ownership over yourself. Sounds about right, but in my case, at age twenty-eight, I felt that my life was under the control of forces beyond me, that there was some grand master pulling the strings, and that, ultimately, someone else was always to blame. When the father planet returns to the first house, you immediately graduate from victim to authority, and—like it or not—become Saturn incarnate.

One of my favorite clients, Mel, hit her first-house Saturn Return, and *hard*. Before Saturn returned to her first house, it completed an intense tour of her twelfth—that dark domain where we process, heal, and ready for our awakening. She got sober, realized that she did not fit the gender she had been assigned, and began her transition. As Saturn hit a new dawn crossing her first house, she declared that she wanted to be a pop star, with ambitions for world domination. The time had come for her debut. I still remember the day I first saw the new her, the exact moment when she strutted into the party as if in slow motion. This person who had been a bit lost, a bit all over the place, was suddenly formed, stomping in, totally owning her radiant embodiment and chosen name. Months later, we were all moshing at her concert, screaming her lyrics of emancipation and revenge, while she beamed down at us from the stage.

I bring up Mel because her first-house Saturn Return, on a very literal level, was about taking form. Having survived the initiatory death and rebirth that closes out the chart, she was ready to not only start over in the first house but to also rip the zodiac out of the heavens and stuff it into her purse. It's her story now. She gets to play God.

When Saturn returns to the first house, your core form, function, and philosophy may be up for reimagining. Look back at photos from your teens and twenties, and you may see a blurry person, a vague entity who isn't quite *there* yet. That won't cut it from this point on, not if Saturn has anything to say about it. You'll have to take the reins, so start by overhauling your confidence and sense of security. To mark her second coming on this planet, Mel landed in platform boots. Get clear on what grounds you, keeps you here, in yourself, in an identity, a body, a purpose. Not to put too much pressure on you, but if we're really to begin a new three-decade cycle, we need it to have a point.

I should also say that planets in your first house may register as people who took on a prominent role in your early development. Saturn, of course, favors the role of the dominating parent figure. In my experience, this plays out in two ways. Often, Saturn here shows up as an overbearing, possibly crushing father archetype, whose presence blocked the healthy development of your ego, personality, and direction. When Saturn returns to the first house, you'll have to metaphorically kill your father (or mother, depending on whose voice reminds you that you're a failure when you're up at three in the morning).

You will have to confront not only the abuse wrought by this devastating presence but also the ways in which you have made yourself small, meek, and even twee so as not to resemble big bad Daddy. Saturn's presence in the first house confirms that you're meant to claim power, to be a shaper, a will, a force. No more hiding or making yourself invisible. Face your parents' flaws and complexities, make contact with your own dangerous drives, and get on with it.

Conversely, and quite commonly, Saturn in the first house indicates a totally absent parent and the need, at a very young age, for the child to take outsize responsibility. Many of my clients undergoing a first-house Saturn Return grew up too early, washing the dishes while Mom was working the night shift, learning that they'd have to teach themselves to drive because Dad wasn't around. After making their own way in the world, they now must reclaim a childhood that has been lost. In short, they have to learn how to have fun.

This form of Saturn Return involves a healthy departure from one's Saturnian makeup. Outside of your duties and responsibilities, who are you? What brings you pleasure? You're stable and set up. Now what? It can be frightening to contemplate what it is you want to do with your life now that the bills are paid and the dishwasher is running.

Opposing the first house of self is the seventh house of others, the mirror through which we let ourselves be seen. When Saturn is at work in your first house, the priority will be more on you. Saturn has no intention of crushing your existing relationships, but rather will help you realize your place as the constant in all of them. There are fundamental questions you need to resolve for yourself so as to be more present for others.

I wish I could say that these reckonings and realizations only come for you at age twenty-eight, but come your midfifties, after devoting yourself to a career, dream, or children, you're once again at that open cliff, considering the ways you've lost a little of yourself along the way and really asking questions about what happens next. The fundamental rules are the same—only this time, you'll have to get even more creative so that you can shake off the outdated roles of parent or capitalist cog that overtook your identity.

Whether you're embracing your inner parent or finally getting some distance from it, when Saturn returns to the first house, you'll experience the liberating—and lonely—realization that your life is your own, that only you can decide what you want, and that the next cycle is yours to write.

Woof. It's a lot of pressure. But it's also power such as you've never dreamed. We're looking over the horizon at the eleven houses to come, at the next thirty years of your life. You just got here. Anything is possible. What do you want to do with it?

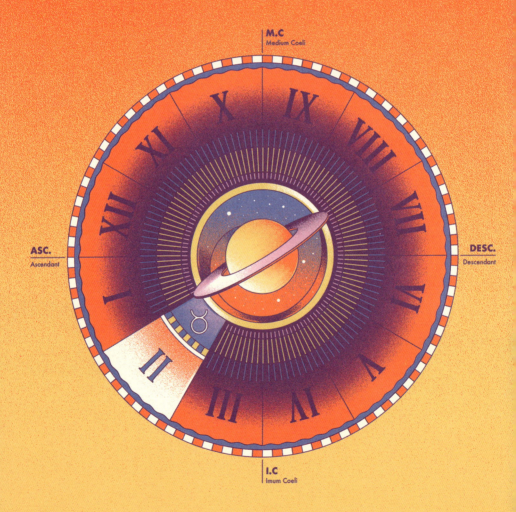

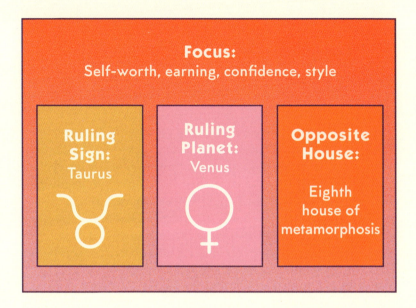

Welcome to the second house of the astrology chart, the domain of possessions and values. This is where you discover the things you own, which, lumped all together, comprise the mosaic of you. I think of this house as your bedroom armoire, which opens up to reveal the items you put on your body every day. Ownership deals with worth, so we're also talking about income, wealth, and the values you possess. So what happens when the grand accountant of the solar system (you know who we're talking about) gets its hands on your tax statements? It's time to make your way in the world and make your own money, without the old dependencies that governed you. When Saturn returns to the second house, you'll learn the true price of freedom.

At some point in everyone's toddlerhood, you start going from giggly cherub to . . . vengeful little tyrant. It's *my* toy. It's *my* Popsicle. It's not fair. But no matter how big a pain in the ass you may be for your parents and playmates, this is a natural means of demarcating your existence, of declaring that you are an autonomous being. That Power Ranger must be yours and yours alone, because without it, who would you be? Whether we're talking toys or real estate holdings, your assets root you to the tangible earth. They're a big part of who you are.

It's considered inelegant, in polite society, to discuss money. That's likely because most of us have a fucked-up relationship with it. You grew up with no money, and you're ashamed of it. You grew up with too much money, and you're ashamed of it. You're broke now and are too embarrassed to ask for help. You've asked your parents for said help, which makes you even more embarrassed. You're following your dream, but you can't pay rent. You're working a soulless job, and it's afforded you a penthouse. How couldn't this be loaded territory?

For Saturn, which acts as a planetary business consultant, the second house is a place of great possibility. Saturn really wants you to feel a sense of order and harmony when it comes to what you do, what you earn, and what you spend it on. The vagueness you feel is holding you back from taking agency. If you're waiting for some big break to save you from having to take responsibility, you're in for a disappointment. It's up to you to update your spending spreadsheet or continue to bear the insult of overdraft fees.

Issues of debting, underearning, and overspending are classics for this house. You may have an "artistic temperament" like me, which means you've shunned money out of fear, not realizing that it could indeed help you to accomplish your dreams. I've also had clients who, having grown up in financial instability, have become overly responsible to the point of miser-dom, fearfully hoarding money but not knowing how to enjoy it. One way or another, this changes with Saturn's arrival.

No discussion of money would be complete without bringing up family, and the ways that our *mispucha* instills in us a core sense of self-worth and entitlement. Yikes. I should mention that opposing the second house is the eighth, the domain of familial inheritance, where we cast off the roles assigned to us within our family of origin. Your finance issues didn't come from nowhere; nor can they be fixed by self-help affirmations alone. You need to get clear on how the economic messaging of your childhood still informs you. As the eighth deals with changing roles in the familial structure, we understand that second-house rehabilitation could spell out liberation for your family ecosystem. As you come into autonomy, old dependencies and narratives are melted away. Everyone can start relating to one another without strings attached.

Consider how dependency, financial or otherwise, led to blurred boundaries and kept you from establishing yourself. Perhaps Saturn here takes the form of a subsuming parent figure who saw you as an extension of themselves. Depending on your parents' sense of boundaries, you may not have been afforded a chance to know where you end and others begin. If, at age twenty-eight, you're wearing outfits that your mother picked out for you and still bound to the family phone plan, and the shared bank account you opened with your dad at age fifteen, you have some tangible work to do toward demarcating your own identity.

This Saturn Return will be a reckoning of independence, of learning how to provide for yourself. You can no longer crawl into your parents' bed when you have a nightmare. You'll have to make yourself tea when you get sick—and you'll have to pay for the honey. Do you believe that you *deserve* security? If your parents had nothing financially, you may have emerged into the world feeling small and incapable of asking for a slice of the pie. Conversely, if your parents had money and used it to dominate you, the same worthlessness may render you totally unprepared to take care of yourself.

I hate to say it, but based on my own second-house Saturn Return, it may behoove you to be broke for this awakening to fully unfold. You may need to be ripped out of complacency, cut off from the udder, fired from the 9–5, or kicked out of the last rent-controlled apartment in the world. In the shock of losing it all, you can begin the comeback. If you can take total ownership over your destiny and develop the tools of accountability necessary to stay sustained and supported, you can climb out of the abyss feeling self-reliant, whole, and solid, no matter what happens to the family finances or global economy.

The second house is square to the eleventh house, which I think of as the domain of ethos and belonging. I mentioned that in the second house, we find all those things that we possess, including values. By the time of your first Saturn Return, many of your friends have found their chosen careers, and some socioeconomic divides have begun to emerge. You have some people in your life who are happily hustling and scraping by, inviting you to their poorly heated apartments to read tarot cards and eat string cheese, while others plan destination weddings and assume you'll have no problem booking airfare and accommodations. Over this Saturn Return, you'll evaluate your career and lifestyle, and as you come into your own sense of personal security, there *should* be social ramifications. Who aligns with what you do? This has nothing to do with moralism; it has to do with embracing your own path and people.

Come your second Saturn Return, it's time for a big assessment of what you've accumulated, what you spend your money on, and who you'd be without all this. To say the least, a garage sale is in order, but on a deeper level, this is a confrontation of complacency. What gives your life value and meaning? If you've put your money into children, or even into your artistic output, you have to find your way back to the center of the picture. Do whatever it takes to pull yourself out of pointless consumption, of greed and wastefulness, of losing yourself in the noise.

Hitting hard in your eighties, a third Saturn Return in this house will involve what you leave behind. These are the items that truly matter to you, and this is who should inherit them. At this point, you are celebrating the life you've led and the character you invested in over the years, and readying yourself to let it go with pride. You've spent a lifetime establishing your worth. Now you get to take with you those intrinsic elements that can't be left behind in a will.

If you do accept Saturn's challenge, if you can face all the ways you've kept yourself small and asked for less than you deserve, if you can gaze into the ruins where a healthy identity should be, then you can start rebuilding. You'll be able to invest in yourself and lay down roots for a real legacy. The new wardrobe, the lease on an apartment, the savings account: They're all yours. You won't need platitudes about asking for more or being yourself, because you'll finally know that you exist. From there, you'll know what you're worth and what you're owed, and you can start asking for it without feeling like a fraud. You're no longer a child, you're a serious participant in the game. Now Saturn can raise the stakes and really bet on you.

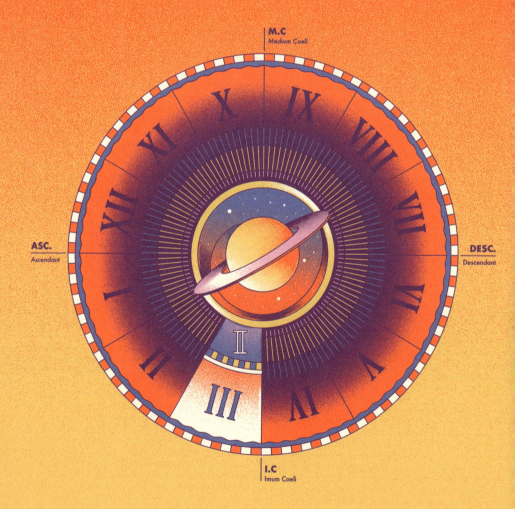

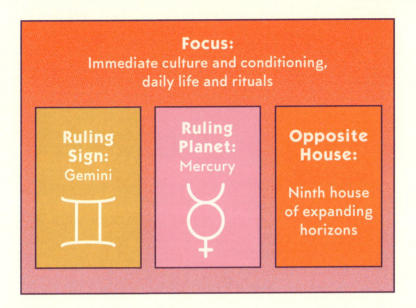

Within minutes of our first meeting, one of my clients informed me that she was destined for the White House. That first reading, for her, was to confirm an intrinsic truth: She was meant for something great. She was going places. And, indeed, her chart had the makings of a legendary senator, president, or rabbi. So why, then, would she be born with Saturn in her third house, the most mundane of places, the one that concerns where we get our coffee in the morning and how well we did in eleventh-grade calculus?

I think of the third house as the realm of culture and conditioning, encapsulating the influences on our immediate reality: what was playing on the radio on your carpool ride to school, the people you talk to every day, the fundamentals of your daily life. This house is a full 180 degrees from the ninth house of travel and expanding horizons. Those big dreams are off in the far future. Here, the focus is on the present. You will consider how the aspects of your day-to-day affect your health, happiness, and future. When Saturn returns to the third house, you're called to rebuild your life from the ground up.

I had a client remark to me—without realizing that I was working on this chapter—that "the trajectory of your life is the sum of your daily practices." That's Saturn for you. Like many of my creative friends, I spent my twenties believing that I'd learn how to take care of myself after I'd *made it*. That ended well. No matter how vast the scale of your ambitions or the shimmering fire of your talent, you can't go anywhere if you don't know how to be good to yourself. Saturn likes routine. It's not that you have to take a crushing, repetitive job to fulfill some sort of cosmic taxation, but think about the firmament that sustains you. What do you need to feel whole when you wake up in the morning?

Located at the base of the chart, the third house informs us of what you're taking in and what feeds you. We are all the product of what's around us. There is a wilting flower effect when it comes to a poorly nourished third house. Exposed to enough light, to fresh air and ideas, we grow. Left in the dark, to the same old coping mechanisms, we sulk. I'm sure you have a friend or two like this. Buy her tickets to the theater, send her a good recipe, get her dancing to the Pointer Sisters, and she comes alive. Take her out of the sun and leave her to her old coping mechanisms—fast food, Instagram, and bad reality TV—and she sinks. Over this Saturn Return, you'll consider those parts of life that have become stagnant, and adopt new routines that feel healthy and nourishing. Maybe you start going to a local church you just discovered and find that you look forward to waking up early on Sunday mornings, that you get something out of ritual and community. Suddenly, you don't miss blacking out every Saturday night with friends you never really liked.

These additions and subtractions will be the bread and butter of your expanding world. Saturn wants you to put down roots in what is real and tangible so that the bigger, epochal changes in your life—love, career, death, etc.—can come and go. You'll still be here, at your Wednesday-night bowling league, feeling grounded and sustained.

I wrote much of this book while Saturn was in my third house. The things that currently bring me the most consistent delight include my Monday-night Zumba class; the panang curry I cooked a few hours ago; my long morning ritual of stretching, praying, meditating, and doing twelve-step work; and the rugelach at my neighborhood café. The rest is all icing on the cake. Two years ago? I was too dissociated to even taste food, too obsessed with *getting through it* (whatever that means) to be able to take a walk around the block. There was always some bigger crisis or opportunity that kept me from being *here*. To get me to stop running toward the horizon and off the cliff, Saturn stripped a lot away. It introduced health crises and threw off career paths. I had no choice but to slow down. It also returned me to delights I'd lost sight of: Dancing. Ice cream. Making the bed every morning. It's not to say that I've cast away all my ambitions, but I understand that my priority must be enriching my experience of *this* moment.

And by the way, there are many, many mornings when I don't want to perform all the rituals, when the meditations feel rote, when I want to burn it all down. But even if it's in a spirit of resentment, I must show up, because I know how fast I'd spiral without these routines to hold me together. If I want to change the ritual, I can. Maybe I'll find something even better.

Because the third house interfaces with our immediate culture, it also deals with how we communicate and interact with the world. Saturn's presence here, then, will involve not only a necessary editing of your social circles but also a rediscovery of your voice. How are you expressing yourself? Back to my client, the one who will someday be our beneficent world leader, I'm curious to see how she learns to shape her message through daily interaction, to introduce herself and hone her pitch to new peers or even adversaries, to sculpt the clay, as it were.

The voice issue and the matter of one's daily routine and rituals all come down to a fundamental question: Are you living your own life? If you're twenty-eight and still talking the way your brothers told you to, back when you were eleven and closeted, maybe it's time to get a vocal coach and let yourself harmonize in a falsetto with George Michael. Or maybe you realize, as your recent migraine symptoms worsen, that scrolling Instagram doesn't make you feel good. What does? If terror rises at the thought of creating a lifestyle that is your own, confront the voice on the other side. Ask yourself if there's something you feel you're betraying by leaving the ranch or the sorority. Why does it feel dangerous to live life on your terms? Maybe someone told you that it was indulgent to have needs. If your parents suffered through soul-numbing jobs and never cultivated their own sense of intentions and interests, they may have sunk the grim into you. It's time to shake it off and do it your way.

I'll try to be delicate here, but if we've learned anything from recent elections, we can see that those with decades of experience are just as vulnerable to outside influence as anyone else. A fiftysomething, or even an eightysomething, can apparently lose their wits if exposed to enough cable news, talk radio, or articles written by bots. And so, when Saturn returns a second or third time, the third house will require the same refreshing as before. You'll have to confront how your life has become brackish and claustrophobic, how you've siloed yourself away from different perspectives, generations, and ideas. The flower will need new soil, or else you'll find you've become a cliché of an angry old man, yelling at the neighborhood kids to get off his lawn. Maybe you should take up Tai Chi or listen to audiobooks while picking up trash in the neighborhood. Do whatever you can to get out of your little head and into the world.

Regarding that ambitious client of mine, she's destined to make it. But through the work of her third-house Saturn Return, she's also set to enjoy her life, to arrive at success with a retinue of kind and trustworthy friends, and to know how to take care of herself when things get rough. She's proved to Saturn that she's not only interested in success but also consistency.

In twelve-step philosophy, the answer for any problem is, inevitably, one day at a time. Many of Saturn's lessons come down to control and how little of it we actually have over the world around us, but the third house is an exception. It represents an invitation to focus on the small stuff. Sometimes, all you can do is water the plants, take out the garbage, and fold the linens. That can be enough to carry you through the great metamorphoses to come. There is no future without care in the present.

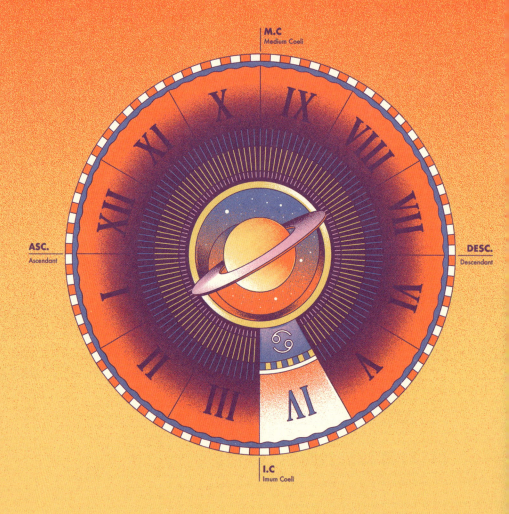

Fourth House

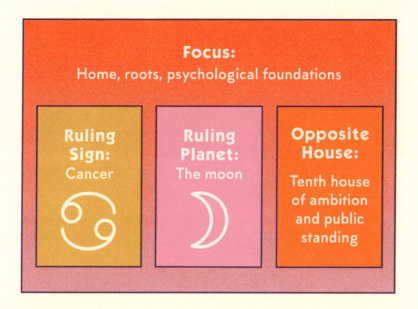

By this point in our journey together, I hope I've demonstrated that nothing written in the stars is set in stone, that everything is up to interpretation, and that even death can be massaged in the language of metaphor. However. You *are* reading a book about Saturn, and we have now reached the fourth house of family. If we're ever to face your daddy, mommy, governess, or piano teacher issues, it's now or never. The fourth house represents the base of the chart, the beating ventricle that pulses life to the other houses. This is Tatooine, the Shire, or, in many cases, the suburban town where Freddy Krueger goes on a killing spree. When Saturn returns to the fourth house, you'll heal your family history and start a new pattern.

Every house is important to the cohesive mosaic of your chart. But the fourth house is something like the root of the tree. It is located at the bottom of the chart, and so its impact reverberates to all the critical angles, namely the first house of self, the seventh house of others, and the tenth house of career. If you've ever found yourself in a relationship with a shadow of your mother, or locked in a joyless career path so as to impress your father, you understand how it all goes back to your origin.

The fourth informs us of our family and our home life, past and present. Here, Saturn will take the form of a parent figure. Ideally, Saturn's presence in the fourth house should speak to the forebear who gave us a sense of inner stability, who paved a foundation upon which we could build.

Ideally. When Saturn returns to the fourth house, you'll have to confront how your Saturnian parent may have missed the mark. Perhaps their monolithic expectations proved impossible to fulfill, crushing you before you could even start. Maybe they were difficult or not present at all. One way or another, some review will be necessary as to what was missing, and where that's led you astray.

The last thing I want to do, in a book about growing up, is absolve you of responsibility, encouraging you to blame your present disasters on something someone else did seventeen years ago. If you're reading this book, then I know you want to move through this, to process it and move on, unshackled from the past. But to really begin a liberated new era, we must take an honest accounting of what was lost, wasted, or lacking the first time around. It's the only way to reckon with all the ways you've overcompensated since.

I'll say this: I arrived at my Saturn Return believing that my childhood had been pristine, that nothing was really wrong, and that any of the blips I was experiencing—mood swings, tantrums, dissociation, sexual acting out, insomnia, overeating, depression, underearning, and so on—must be caused by some random chemical imbalance. Or maybe it was me. I must be inherently bad. Oy. It was inevitable that I'd have to creep down the basement stairs, look through the photo albums, and contemplate where this all really came from. Once I understood the story—or, at least, more of it—I could address what I'd inherited, what had been done to me, and what was mine to take responsibility for in the present.

And by the way, Saturn doesn't expect you to solve it all here. Your chart, like this book, is one hell of a Choose Your Own Adventure story: At different times in life, you're called to different houses and their specific assignments. Consider the eighth house of familial inheritance, or the twelfth house of repressed history. You'll deal with these core issues from different vantage points. And remember, we're dealing with Saturn here, not another planet, so your mission parameters are quite specific. If Pluto were to hit your fourth house, I'd be sending you on a psychedelic voyage through endless generations, communing with ancestors from three hundred years ago to reset your familial karma. But this is Saturn, the planet of structure and accountability. We are trying to rebuild the constitution of your cognitive reality by addressing the immediate environment in which you were raised. That should be plenty to work on over the next three years.

Of course, some form of therapy will be essential for this transit. As this is the domain of the home, we're trying to locate the damages in your foundation. Beyond the healing of ancient wounds, we want to get a sense of your gaps in processing, the places where you didn't receive adequate love. Internal Family Systems (IFS) creates a language around our inner parents and children, allowing us to interface with those repressed and hurt parts, creating a balanced whole. Cognitive and dialectic behavioral therapies help you to engage with the world in the day-to-day. If you were indeed raised by wolves, we can teach you to speak to your fellow man. If you can learn how to nourish yourself now, in the ways you never were as a child, you'll be able to take on the role of provider and recognize your parents for what they are. Or, as my mother always said self-deprecatingly, "I'm doing my best, which isn't very good!" As you see one another differently, there's a possibility for friendship to emerge, or at least respect. This will be useful in the years to come.

On the topic of home, we're not only referring to your childhood digs in the suburbs and the basement futon where you lost your virginity. It's time to address your current lodgings and the ways they either reflect or suppress the luminous galaxies of potential within you.

Of course, I could go on a tirade about cleanliness, godliness, and how the way one sanitizes their commode reveals all you need to know about their upbringing. But let's skip the meltdown and go a bit deeper. Does the home you're in feel like your own? Did you pick out this apartment because it sang to you, or because you felt like it would incur the fewest passive-aggressive comments from your mother? Did you black out at IKEA while buying the furniture, or do the pieces here feel cultivated?

It can take a long time to feel like you deserve a space of your own and that what's on the walls and in the spice rack are genuine reflections of you. If you don't feel ready to put down roots, that's fine, but by taking even the smallest steps toward a tangible sense of resonance—laying out a rug or cleaning the refrigerator—you are working toward feeling safer.

It's likely that a move is in order, come this Saturn Return. Maybe you showed up in the big city five years ago, desperate to prove yourself, and you've realized that, having healed your familial *mishegoss*, you really miss your charming hometown. Or perhaps a volcanic breakup has forced you out of your shared abode and out into the open. Love and real estate have a way of going together, and falling apart. Jettisoned from your couples' prison, you now get to discover your own rhythm. Moves are always difficult. But they also offer closure. Don't bother with a storage locker or half measures. You're being challenged to end a chapter definitively.

Once you've worked through the tests of the fourth house, you become Saturn incarnate, paving the way for your own home and family built on a sturdy foundation. Whether you're parenting your inner children or buying a bunk bed for your twins, it's on you now to play the role of mama bear. And good news: You're not necessarily cursed to repeat the mistakes of your parents. Or at least, when you do, you can address it and keep going. The point is, you're free to make your own kind of family now.

By the time of your second or even third Saturn Return, you will likely have invested quite a few shekels in your real estate. Reviewing your four-figure air-conditioning bills for the month, you realize that this McMansion no longer brings you happiness. Perhaps the kids are moving out or they're coming back, grandkids in tow. The function of your residence must change to honor your present circumstances. This will also be a time to reflect on your role in the matrix. As you experience changes in health, you realize that it's time to make amends and bury old grudges. Maybe it's time to pick up the phone and call that sibling you haven't spoken to since the "event" at Thanksgiving five years ago. If there's something left undone, something that could bring you peace at the dinner table, now's the time.

This assignment calls for bravery. But it's worth it. By facing the specters of your childhood, you'll access the scorching cauldron of generative possibility that the fourth house promises. In one lifetime, we're not always able to heal the wounds of family. But by showing up, you're signaling to Saturn that you're ready for a new dynamic. Hold fast, and you may wake up one day no longer feeling like a Roald Dahl character. Finally, we're out of the orphanage. You've made it home.

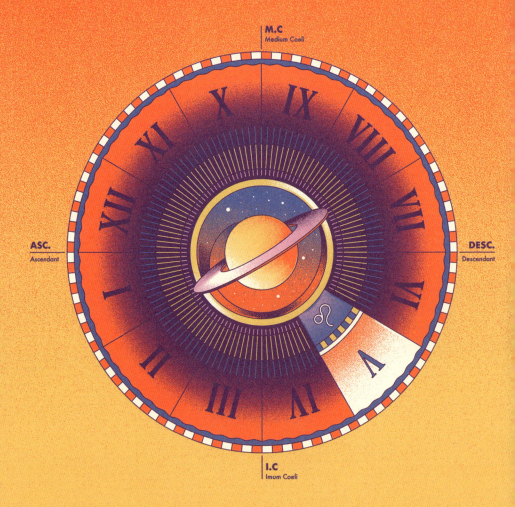

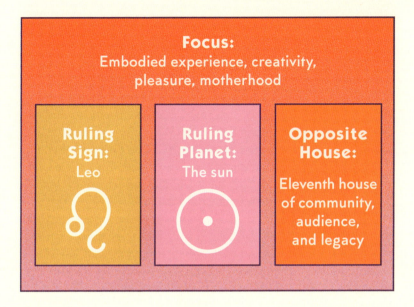

Dare I say it, but have we arrived at the house of fun? Traditionally, the fifth house is thought of as the domain of pleasure, creativity, and even romance. Of course, our analysis will yield more nuanced understandings, but this being a book about Saturn, we should learn to take it where we can get it.

If we were to liken your soul's journey to that of Superman, those first four houses largely concern your arrival to this planet. The rocket has crashed in Kansas, the nice farm people have taken you in, and you're on your way. House five, then, is when you discover your superpowers. I refer to the fifth house as the house of embodied experience, where we discover what it is you're meant to do: your talents, gifts, and creative contributions to the world. We also learn what it is you like to do while you're renting a time-share in this mortal coil. In the fifth, the planet of definition wants you to identify your passion. When Saturn returns to the fifth house, you'll discover what you want to do with your life and take responsibility for it.

We are nearly complete with the first half of the chart—the personal sector—and will soon be negotiating the terms of entrance into public life. At this point, Saturn needs you to be clear on what it is you're here to do, so that you can be put to the highest benefit to humanity. The fifth house directly opposes the eleventh house of community and audience. Superman masters his powers and gets clear on what he's fighting for: truth and justice. In no time, he's inspiring other superheroes to take to the skies. There is something that only you can offer the human race, and if you can't take responsibility as its custodian, the world may be at a critical loss.

To begin, we need to figure out what your *thing* is. The fifth house is known as the domain of motherhood, referring to all things we create, from children to very bad screenplays. Perhaps you were raised by subsuming parents, the types who saw you as an extension of themselves. Come age twenty-seven, you may struggle to define those joys and vocations that are *yours* and not *theirs*. This Saturn Return may function as a second childhood, a time to find those activities that bring you delight.

And what about your calling? Our cultural heroes yap at us, ad nauseam, to believe in our dreams. But you may feel too underwater to even know what it is you want. Fear not: Saturn has this one covered. It's likely that you're already doing it on some level. While organizing your best friend's death march of a baby shower, you find yourself arranging a diaper cake that would make Michelangelo bow and supplicate. Your 9–5 job may be punishing, but at the annual Hanukkah karaoke party, you come alive as the MC and find that you're a natural with a mic. Pay attention: You're never that far from yourself.

And besides some divine vocation, you may discover things that you just enjoy doing. Perhaps you keep your corporate desk job but spend all the vacation days hiking the mountains of Bhutan. That will mean skipping the annual family yacht trip in Newport. You'll be met with derision. They don't get it. They don't get *you* anymore. But it makes you happy.

If you really don't know what it is you're meant to do or what it is that makes you happy, it doesn't mean you're in trouble or helplessly dull. The fact that you're willing to ask, that something in you isn't content to watch the game and dissociate until you're dead, means that Saturn has found a willing cocreator in you. Now's the best part: the experimentation. Try out books like Dr. Alex Schiller's *Never Sleep Alone* or Julia Cameron's *The Artist's Way*. They provide concrete prompts for how to kindle a relationship with yourself. Dress to the nines, grab a book, and go sit alone at a fancy bar. Put on sunglasses and walk to the museum. Devote time every morning to writing about your dreams and observations. This will require guts and humility. But results will come if you're willing to part with expectations.

Do you have the freedom to pursue interests and desires? And, if you are to really take them seriously, consider who they'd threaten. Like the second house of self-worth, the fifth demands a declaration. Clark Kent, however mundane he'd like to be, must at some point take to the skies. As you start to get curious about, well, *you*, Saturn will call for yet another accounting of relationships. The people around you should be excited by your evolving pursuits, asking questions that stimulate you. They should have their own passions. You'll want to develop an inner circle that propels you rather than keeps you in stifling complacency.

Of course, this being a Saturn Return in the fifth house, you'll have a lot to learn about discipline. What do you need to deliver your novel to paper? As I mentioned, the fifth house concerns not only artistic creations but also human ones . . . namely babies. Whatever it is you're bringing to term, Saturn wants in. Decide what sort of space or support you need to feel engaged and like yourself so you don't burn out.

That space will be necessary to keep you from getting overly attached to your project . . . or person. As you come to be a creator, you'll have to learn the tenets of healthy depersonalization. You don't want to be one of *those* parents, screaming like a lunatic at their fourth grader's Little League scrimmage. Perhaps, after years of agony and sacrifice, you've completed the manuscript of your fantasy novel. You'll have to find a way to handle the rejection to come. Are you your child, your gallery exhibition, your album—or are they things that move *through* you, to be released into the world, to mean something different to themselves and others?

Embodied experience. A few years ago, I organized a weeklong time-share with friends in Fire Island. Everyone seemed to have a good time except for me, the tyrannical house mother, resentfully scrubbing the floors, scorning the "children" for any deviation they made from the plan. Even the acid trips were scheduled. Yikes. By the pool, at the beach, on the dance floor: I was anywhere but in my own body.

Saturn is the god of control. It's time for you to give it up. This date, this wedding, this solo show—they're meant to be fun. Saturn needs you to be able to have experiences unburdened by crippling shame and perfectionism. This is where a supportive cohort of other creative, engaged people comes in: a writer's group, a knitting circle, even just a few other moms who are new to this journey. It will also require the confrontation with your real or internalized pageant parents, with those forces who judge you, who have made it hard for you to have a good time and not take yourself so seriously. No matter the outcome, Saturn needs you to be able to pick up again and move on to the next project, not hide in a cave and disappear forever.

Your movie may not be nominated for best picture. Your dream date may be a bad kisser. Your friends might get famous, while you still take dog-walking gigs to make rent. And, just as probably, your creative endeavors may yield great satisfaction, even joy. Your dreams could indeed come true. Trust me: I've seen it happen. Either way, positive or negative, none of these experiences are you. They happen to, through, and around you. You're the engine, the generator, the conduit, the keeper. Only you know what you need to stay centered and not get taken for a ride.

A few years ago, I saw Alanis Morissette perform live, at a twenty-fifth-anniversary celebration of her debut album, *Jagged Little Pill*. The stadium was packed with fans now approaching middle age, whose coming-of-age had been shaped by this album. Alanis, years from the angst of her early music, was solid as diamond. Since *Jagged Little Pill*, she'd explored the world and made beautiful, diverse music. Onstage, she was able to channel *Jagged Little Pill*, to help us all connect to its meaning and feeling, but it was clear that she wasn't stuck in it. She had the healthy distance to be able to head-bang, wail, and shriek with rage, all without losing herself in the maelstrom. She was whole, in herself. That's mastery.

Come your second or even third Saturn Return, the sacrifice will be the same, but the stakes will be higher. You may have executive-produced a TV show that means something to millions. Now it's been canceled—either by the network or by the moralistic masses. Or, signing the divorce papers after two decades of marriage, you realize that you don't know how to spend a night at home alone. Like my heroine Diane Lane in *Under the Tuscan Sun*, you'll have to embrace humiliation: as you join a group of gay men on a tour bus through Italy; as you take yourself out, alone, for gelato; as you renovate the kitchen in your villa. It's time to change your attitude and throw yourself at something new.

I opened this chapter with the boy from Krypton coming out of the rocket. Given a chance to drink in the sunlight and try on spandex, he goes from orphan to farmboy to supergod, blasting through the skies, immortal, indestructible, indefatigably optimistic. When Saturn returns to the fifth house, you'll claim your liberation. Your most elevated self is ready to take to the skies, to tap into that solar power that never burns out. If there's something in you that suspects the possibility of *more*, then you're already on your way. Saturn will teach you how to fly. You just need to take the first jump.

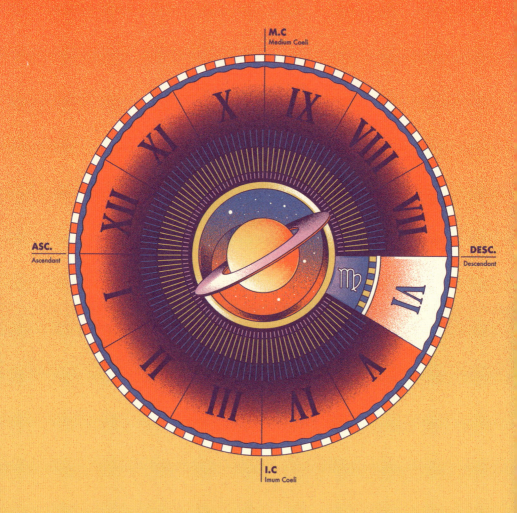

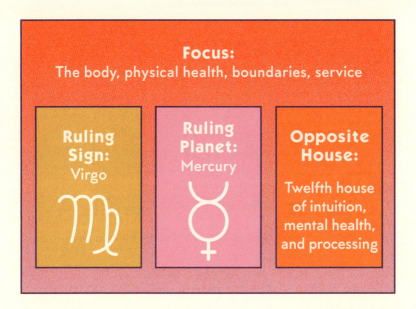

We have arrived at a critical turning point in the chart, the threshold between the personal and the inter-relational. The first six houses concern the self. Over the last twelve years or so, Saturn has slowly restructured every aspect of your waking experience, from money to family. When Saturn crosses into the seventh house, and into the public half of your chart, it's showtime. Right now is your final chance to check your hair and makeup before you take the stage.

The sixth is the house of the body and its needs. When Saturn crossed the fifth house, we encountered our divine talents and began to inhabit our bodies—and even enjoy them. In the fifth house, you fell in love with yourself; in the seventh, you'll let the world fall in love with you. But someone's got to protect you as you head out into the world, ensuring that you're healthy and safe, and that your gifts aren't being exploited. The negotiations to come involve the concrete aspects of your physical existence.

When Saturn returns to the sixth house, you'll learn to respect your needs and demand others do the same.

In the sixth house, Saturn needs to know what your body can handle and how it can best be put to use. We're dealing with the actual logistics of labor and how your lifestyle can either fuel or sabotage the highest expression of your potential. These matters are separate from the second house of finances and the tenth house of career and ambition. This may be the most practical house of all. Saturn's presence here centers your body as the creative generator, its tangible needs essential to your success.

"If you love what you do, you'll never work a day in your life." Yeah, right. Ad executives on Madison Avenue came up with that one, and here you are, already exhausted in your late twenties, having hustled, grinded, scraped, and clawed to get ahead, whatever that means. When Saturn returns to the sixth house, you're offered a chance to reappraise what it is you do, how you can most efficiently do it, and how you deserve to be compensated. No more unpaid internships or demeaning assistant jobs. It's time for you to call the shots.

In the sixth house, Saturn teaches essential lessons about limits, the type that signal an end to twentysomething party-girl behavior. You're learning how to take care of yourself, and signaling that you can do so over any flux of career and fortune. If you've been singing at local bar shows for years but were to be picked up tomorrow by a record label and sent on a yearlong tour, could you be counted on to get enough sleep, eat well, and not burn out? What do you do to ensure you don't lose your voice on the road? What drugs would you say no to?

Or, *ahem*—let's say you're an astrologer and intuitive. When I started, I took on too many readings, not knowing how badly I'd crash without a break. Years into my practice, I'm still figuring out how many clients I can meet in a week, how much I should charge per reading, and what is necessary to recover the next day. In working out the logistics of what I do, I have to deal with matters of money, physical stamina, and time. These choices affect everything, and I usually feel best when I've done the least rather than pushed myself over the edge.

Saturn's magic word is *no*. Say it, and you'll feel the rocks and stones and mountains gather around you. This won't always be easy, especially if you've been conditioned to believe that what you have is not worth much, or that you have to give it away for approval or affection. But when you make the declaration—no, I'm not going to work for the promise of publicity; no, I'm not going to man the cotton candy booth at the carnival; no, I don't want to do an improv set at 1:00 a.m. in Jersey City—it's a psychedelic affirmation of your existence and your commitment to yourself.

So what does this look like for you? It doesn't matter if your brother works forty-hour shifts in the ER. If you require nine hours of sleep a night to feel like you have a fighting chance, that's just fine by Saturn. It's when you play by someone else's terms that you get into trouble.

This being the house of the body, here's where we get into health, so let me get this out of the way. I don't know your life, nor do I propose to have a holistic write-off for the illnesses you experience. Sometimes bad things just happen, and often, Western medicine has the solution. However, some health crises can be attributed to lifestyle choices or to deeper factors. As Liz Greene writes in *Saturn*: "Illness is always a reflection of imbalance, even if we assign it a purely physical origin."

The sixth house directly opposes the twelfth house of intuition and repressed emotion. Based on just about every reading I've ever done, there's *always* a connection; as ever, the call is coming from inside the house. Saturn will push the agenda. You can't keep living like this, forcing it down, pretending it's not there. Old trauma tells its story on your skin, in your nightmares, through pains and maladies. Current stressors make you pay attention. I'm not saying that this Saturn Return necessitates some bizarre disease meant to teach you a lesson about being present. But if you think you can either stuff it away, numb it out, or romanticize living dangerously, the party is coming to a sharp end.

Saturn is not auditing you for the sake of productivity. It's trying to help you live longer, doing what's right for you. If you're willing to stop resisting and perhaps part with some of the less-than-nourishing aspects of your life, Saturn's tour through your sixth house will reveal to you the most pleasurable ways you'd like to live. You discover what happens when you're not pushed to extremes. You find time. You begin to take in the scenery.

Saturn's great love is efficiency, and its operations in the sixth house are meant to determine how you can be put to service and in what capacity. This is what you and your body can take on, in these conditions. By establishing the boundaries of what you have to offer, you'll be more available to give it your all. Things won't be coming at you now that you have a built-in filter. Write down your nonnegotiables for a potential mate and partner, and you won't waste your time with half-assed dates. When a promising candidate comes along, you show up sparkling. If that nonprofit can meet your wage demands for that executive director gig, you'll be in the trenches, eager and excited, ready to help the cause. The key concept here is *consolidation*: learning how to retain your presence, keeping your gifts to yourself, until the right opportunity arrives. This may shock you, but you're worth it.

Sometimes, with Saturn in the sixth house, we encounter the opposite: not the one who gives it all away, but the one who never steps out in the first place. We all have a friend like this: crackling with talent yet still waiting for that perfect moment. You want to shake her and tell her to put up her solo show even if it's not perfect, to get that first tattoo, to try out bangs even if she'll regret them. Here, we encounter consolidation to the point of constipation. You don't want to be waiting in the wings forever. Once again, it comes down to boundaries. Only you know what you need to feel safe in the world. But inevitably, you'll have to make adjustments out in the wild. You can't stay shut in forever.

You don't need a brilliant astrologer to tell you this, but as you age, questions of limitation and health only take more prominence. Every Saturn aspect to the sixth house—that includes squares from the third and ninth houses, oppositions from the twelfth, and returns in your midfifties and eighties—will involve a conversation about your body and its limits. That means, astrologically speaking, that you're due for a cosmic checkup at least every seven years. Imagine, at age twenty-eight, taking those critical first steps toward feeling OK more of the time: a one-hour walk every day at sunset, phones off before bedtime, a two-drink maximum at the bar. You'll regret pushing yourself too far. You'll never regret working less. No one expects you to become a vegan bodhisattva overnight, but anything done with a sense of compassion and care will be appreciated by future incarnations.

A sixth-house Saturn Return elevates you from passivity to mastery. You know what is required for you to not only endure but also succeed. You are securing safe passage for Saturn through the next phase of your chart.

Come ages fifty-five and eighty-four, you'll have to fine-tune your lifestyle once again. Your anxiety about how your kids are raising their own children is literally causing you heart palpitations. Changes in health force you to reconsider how you've been eating your whole life. After staying shut in the house since your spouse's death, your doctor commands you to start walking around the neighborhood. Some baggage has piled up, and your somatic system can't bear the weight anymore. It's on you to know what needs to be changed.

At stake here is the command to know thyself. Your shape defined, the rest of the world can know you, respect you, love you, and support you in taking your place of service and satisfaction. Saturn loves to play the role of sensei or coach in your cinematic training montage. Get in fighting shape so that you can show up to the arena, a master in your own right.

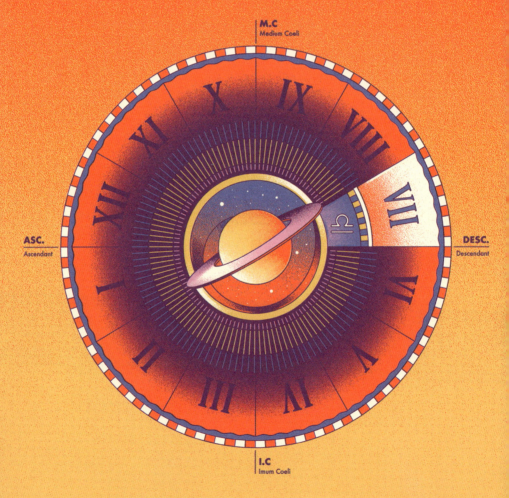

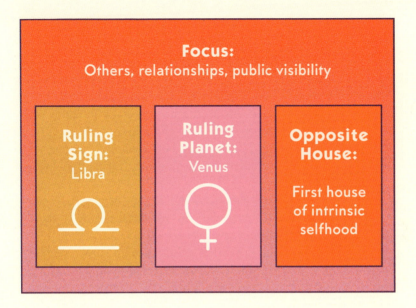

If the first house of intrinsic selfhood introduced us to our protagonist (you), then its opposite, the seventh house of others, rounds out the cast. Here is where we encounter the relationships that will launch us far beyond our origins. But finding the right people requires work. When Saturn returns to the seventh house, the relationship edit is on.

The wheel of the chart is divided in two halves, with the first six houses of the zodiac lining the bottom. This is our vulnerable underbelly: The houses here concern where we come from and what we brought with us. But once we hit the seventh house, we're crossing into the top half of the chart, the bright and busy domain of public life: contacts, community, and the interconnected messiness of people. If we view the chart as a clock, with the first house representing dawn, its opposing house, the seventh, arrives at dusk. Enough with the inner development: It's time for happy hour.

The seventh is regarded, rather infamously, as the house of marriage and relationships. Yet it concerns all aspects of public visibility. Ruled by Libra and Venus, it's the arena of social graces. Katniss Everdeen is ready for her first interview on Capitol TV; Cinderella ditches the dusty rags and shows up at the banquet, ready to scoop up the hottest trade in sight. This is where we come into the view of others and begin to launch forward together. These others may be anyone we engage with intimately: friends, collaborators, mentors, therapists, lovers, and—my favorite—nemeses.

When meeting with clients in the throes of this particular transit, I have to be delicate with my wording, but the facts are these: Saturn will be putting all your relationships through the ringer. We've established that this is the house of public visibility, so we'll have to get clear on what you're seeing in others and what you're letting them see in you. There are necessary questions you've been afraid to ask about the people in your life. Now you don't have a choice.

This Saturn Return won't just involve refreshing your dating profile; you're being called to liberate your relationships from the psychic debris of the past. The seventh house sits at a 90-degree angle, or square, from the fourth house of roots and family. We know that Saturn often manifests in the form of the father archetype: stern, harsh, domineering, unforgiving. From the jump, we have a lot to consider. Namely, are you dating your father? If you are indeed in a relationship when Saturn returns to the seventh house, you'll have to look long and hard at your dearly beloved and contemplate which figures of parental authority cast shadows over them. By examining the deeper influences that affect your choices in lovers and confidants, you can come out from under the grip of unconscious forces. As you dig the roots out of the earth, you'll make way for new life.

Does that mean everyone is getting ripped out? Does Saturn's arrival in the seventh house automatically trigger heartbreak and despair? Certainly not. In the seventh house, Saturn aims to strengthen, repair, and invest in your relationships. Remember, this planet cannot destroy *that which is built to endure*. Saturn will likely strain your relationships, but if you can create new modes of dialogue and lock down iron boundaries, you'll be set for decades to come. Imagine if those legendary bandmates had talked through their respective issues *before* going on that fateful, devastating yearlong tour; if the crown prince had told his wife-to-be that he was in love with someone else. What if you didn't fall into relationships but engaged with them intentionally?

Much of the work of boundary-building is ours to do. But as ruling sign Lady Libra's eyes are covered, so, too, are we blind to those relationships that have run their course. Saturn is the lord of time; he doesn't care about moral or sentimental attachments. Sometimes a relationship is over because it's over.

But usually, you know when you need to cut the cord. Perhaps it's your roommate from freshman year, who wants you to be her maid of honor even though you only speak once a year. The boyfriend from your midtwenties, who has slid from charming insouciance to rabid alcoholism. Your senior manager, who will land you that raise any minute now, so long as he can make thinly veiled remarks about your physical appearance at liberty.

The seventh house arranges the company you'll keep for the rest of your life. And Saturn doesn't allow excess passengers to weigh down the ship. If you are unable to part from the clearly deleterious influences in your life—be it out of guilt or a gluttony for punishment—Saturn will introduce crises to throw them overboard. Oh, the breakup will be ghastly in the moment, sure, but give it three months. Your load will be so lightened, your life so open to new and bona fide bonds, you won't believe you ever lasted so long dragging that burden.

With Saturn in the seventh house, we often encounter older lovers who teach us a thing or two, or, better yet, the right mentors and masters to take us under their wing. These figures will be defined by hardness—whether it's their physical presence or in the enforcement of their methods. You've had plenty of benign, frictionless friendships and long-term love affairs lacking any propulsive spark. Where has all the conflict-free cushioning gotten you? Any pop upstart can hire a yes-man producer. A real diva wants someone in the recording room to tell her the truth and push her to be her best.

A second seventh-house Saturn Return involves a relational resetting for the next phase of your life. Perhaps your children are now adults, or the community of your earlier years has gone in different directions. Relationships from previous eras must evolve with this next chapter of your life. If you and your beloved were once crazed young lovers and then devoted parents, discuss what you want to be now. Maybe you want to be mates on a cruise ship, or Scrabble partners, or something else. But you have to talk it through so that you're not playing out a relationship dynamic from the past.

By your third Saturn Return, you will have taken on the role of Saturn in your family and friendships. You will have to take responsibility for the impacts you've had on others, be it as a guiding influence or crushing parent figure, or both. It's time for them to work out their seventh-house issues with you, and for you to listen, so that all things can be equal in your final years.

By the time Saturn exits your seventh house, you'll know your own score: the codependencies, the mommy issues, the ways you blew it in the past, and all the times you gave your power away, consciously or unconsciously. If that sounds bleak, you're missing the point. Ask any thirtysomething about dating in their twenties, and they'll tell you: It sucked. Only when they'd crossed out of childish romantic fantasies and uninspired sex could they start to channel the chemistry and locate real connection. When this transit ends, you'll be ready to really begin and to find the ones who can cruise with you until the bitter end.

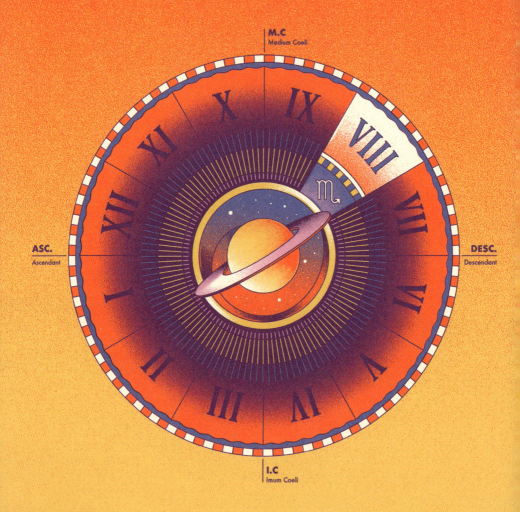

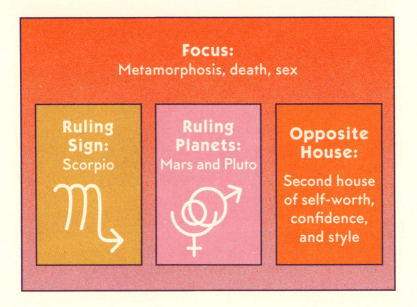

Commonly known as the "house of death," the eighth sends my clients into terror. Originally ruled by Scorpio and arriving just beyond the halfway point of the chart, the eighth house acts as a psychedelic initiatory checkpoint, where your previous identity melts away, a rebirth necessary before the relaunch. Certainly, Saturn has its work cut out for it here. When Saturn returns to the eighth house, you'll release yourself from the roles you've played and embrace the death of your old life.

I should slow down and offer a little context on the death issue before we really get into it. Saturn just passed through the seventh house of others, where we encountered those defining mates who are poised to stick around. Now, as the relationships get serious, they become the vehicles to those critical life cycle events: marriage, parenthood, and death. At the strip club to celebrate your bachelorette party, you kiss your single life goodbye. Smoking a cigar outside the delivery room, you realize that *you're* Daddy now. Reading over your mother's will after her passing, you understand that you've ascended to the role of family matriarch; ready or not, the buck stops with you.

I refer to the eighth house as the house of metamorphosis. Consider initiatory rites in nearly all societies: Bar Mitzvahs, confirmations, receiving tribal tattoos. Here, we mark the definitive, no-going-back transformation from one self to another. These will go down in the eighth house. For Saturn, the planet of adulthood, the agenda must often be forced, and the transformation, once embraced, can be dramatic and rather dazzling.

Remember that the zodiac is a cycle, and we're not yet near the end of the revolution. After the eighth house, we truly go beyond what you've known, into domains of community, travel, higher learning, career expansion, and spirituality. If you're still cleaving to childish identifications or a limited sense of self, Saturn's return to the eighth house will function as basic training, a cleansing of who you were so that you can be sent on your way.

Algorithm culture forces us to pick identities: dog dad, cabaret queen, board game geek. These have a way of getting to be restrictive. Many of us arrive at our Saturn Return believing that *this* is what we are. *I'm a writer, I came to New York to be a writer, and nothing's going to stop me from being a writer.* OK. But what if you're that and more? We adopt roles as a means of coping, of making a linear way through the chaos and uncertainty of childhood and young adulthood. This presents an issue for Saturn, who doesn't really want you to be anything or anybody. Ideally, by the end of your Saturn Return, you'll have ditched the titles and come to a happy neutral, ready to await orders for your next assignment. So the "death" required with an eighth-house Saturn Return is of the self you once marked as definitive. Maybe you're not a writer. Maybe you're a woodworker. Maybe you *are* a writer but not the kind you thought you were. I have no doubt that it will all come together beautifully in the end, but first, a parting will be necessary.

The eighth house marks a descent into the underworld, into those dark domains where the light of day cannot reach. I can assure you that Saturn has big plans for you in the years to come, but it's likely that you'll be the last to know. Your job here is not to plan for what comes next, but to fully make peace with who you were and what you've lost. This is the same with the happier crossings as well. No matter how hard you plan your "big" day, what comes after the wedding cake is a vast unknown, a shared project between two people, the form of which will change as the years go by. For now, it's on you to make closet space and put thought into the parameters of your *ketubah*.

Of course, Saturn being the father archetype, a return to the eighth house can mark the death of a parent. After the finances have been sorted and the *shiva* has been sat through, one must grieve the loss of their fixed role and step into the vacant seat left behind at the head of the table. This transition can play out as a power struggle, either consciously or unconsciously. It was Saturn, remember, who devoured his children to prevent them from usurping him, and his son Jupiter who inevitably escaped his father's bowels, freed his siblings, and led the generational uprising. And so Saturn's presence in the eighth house often points to a restrictive, overshadowing parent, one who keeps us imprisoned in their reality, their wishes, their world order. Metaphorically speaking, this Saturn Return, you'll have to kill your father.

Here's where the eighth house gets interesting, or, shall I say, more interesting. Along with death, this is known as the house of sexuality. Of course, sex provides as powerful and metamorphic an initiatory experience as any tribalistic rite, as we meld into another and part with childhood once and for all. Our sexual expression should terrify our parents; it marks a total loss of innocence and the declaration of our desires, our agency, our full and fearsome embodiment.

I often recommend that my clients find the safest, cleanest dungeon orgy in their neighborhood and see what happens when they cross into the underworld. Sexual awakening is contingent on anonymity; at the bathhouse, you leave your name behind at clothes-check. Who are you, really, when the roles have been relinquished? For many of us, it is here, as we tap into unknown powers, as the werewolf is unleashed, that we confront the shackles placed on us by familial expectation and often abuse. Through sex, we face our parents, and, like Jupiter escaping from Saturn's bowels, we release our repressed inner god.

When Saturn returns to the eighth house, sex will inevitably be on the table. I've had clients with this placement who have kept themselves complacent, smiling and harmless, so as not to threaten the rule of a monolithic parent. Sometimes we encounter marathon monogamists who take shelter in sexless relationships. This Saturn Return introduces the drug trips, three-ways, or familial clashes meant to force them out of extended childhood. By zipping on the latex and facing those desires you once deemed too dangerous to explore, you leave the suburbs behind and accept the consequences of agency and adulthood.

By the way, I've also had the opposite: sexually liberated clients who have perhaps built a persona on the dance floor or music-festival tent. They're looking for something more subtle. The metamorphosis is the same: Who you were, and what you were responding to, is no longer relevant. You just *are*.

My issue with coming-out narratives is the one-and-done approach to personal awakening. In reality, we are destined to come out of many closets in life, and our sexuality should be ever evolving. For now, Saturn's transit through your eighth house is meant to fast-track you out of every closet door, like that chase scene in *Monsters, Inc.*, so that you may enter the ninth house a present and open being, ready for your new roles in the cycle to come.

From what I've observed, this crossing is no less intense come your second Saturn Return. By this point, we've experienced more loss, likely having had to clean out the homes of our dead loved ones, only to return to our careers and wonder, *What now?* If your kids have moved out of the house and moved on, you're faced with the silence, and ambivalence, of what you want to do with the next thirty years. As stated, we're peering over a grand horizon, nearing arrival in your ninth house of expanding horizons, study, and spirituality. Anything is possible. So turn your child's bedroom into a pottery studio, set up a shrine to your dearly departed, make new friends who didn't come from the carpool line, and celebrate all that you did this last go-round. You may not be ready to start over just yet, but as with all Saturnian affairs, the countdown is already underway.

Believe me, I never thought I'd be an astrologer. I had a set path, and I wanted everyone in the world to know about it. No deviations were allowed. But to get here, wherever here is, some dreams had to be surrendered, others had to be integrated, while a few more remain to be sorted out. I look back at who I was before Saturn returned and think, *You really were clinging on tight, weren't you?* I'm not saying it's easy to let it all go, to say yes to the obliteration of all that you've ever known. But show up for this one, and you'll be game for anything, ready to go where the Fates lead you, no longer resisting your path but kicking back and enjoying the ride. Trust that Saturn has a plan for you, and that it might be infinitely better than the one you'd set for yourself.

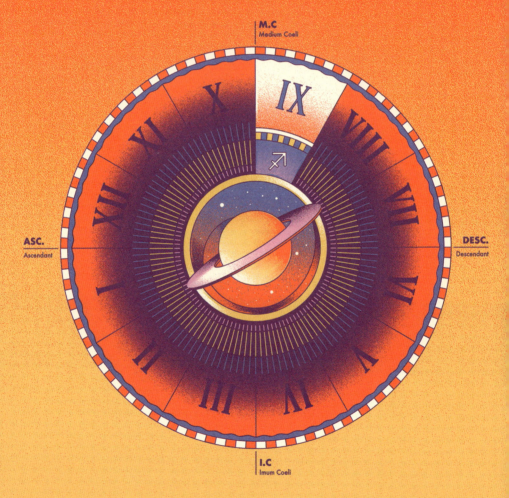

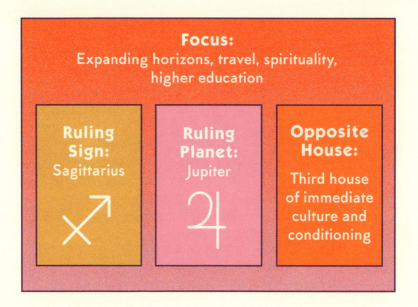

The ninth house of expanding horizons is rarely dull. By this point in the saga of the chart, we're really cooking with gas. Much of the inner metamorphosis has been faced; now we let the finger of fate point us where we're meant to go. The ninth is meant to send us beyond the world of what is known, to thrust us into new and stimulating environs: faraway voyages, spiritual journeys, and academic challenges. Naturally, these sort of karmic relocations require one to surrender control of their destiny. Can you guess where Saturn comes in?

When Saturn returns to the ninth house, you will break with the limiting beliefs that have kept your life small. As soon as Saturn arrives here, it's certain that everything is about to get much bigger, whether you can handle it or not. Your little reality is in for a big shake-up.

The ninth house is known as the house of travel, and indeed it represents the trip necessary to reach the tenth house, our career peak. We get clear on what you need to learn; what skills you need to develop; and which institutions, unions, or guilds you need to get in with. Essentially, where must you go *beyond* yourself? This should be an exciting—and humbling—chapter, as once again you become a student of the world. But if your worldview is limited, you won't have very far to go, nor will you land in a very different place from where you started.

In terms of tarot correspondences, I liken the ninth house to the Three of Wands, which depicts an emperor gazing over an open vista, considering which land to conquer next, à la Alexander the Great. Anything is possible. Sounds nice, and yet, from the beginning, we tend to get in our own way, to cloud our view of the sun with our preconditioned assumptions.

I was once talking to a friend who was about to sign her first book deal, a biography of a very famous, recently deceased public figure. "You know," she said, "nobody reads books anymore. I probably won't make any money from this." It appeared that my friend had presumed not only how her book would perform but also how the entire publishing industry operates. Saturn wields its scythe at the time of harvest, reaping the fields when the time is right. My friend was cutting herself down before the contract was even signed.

Now, to be clear, I do this to myself about five hundred times a day, and often require a friend or paid professional to remind me that I'm setting stakes that don't exist. I stop myself from trying new things because I have an idea in my head about how it *will* go, and usually the idea involves me being humiliated in the town square. This ability to hijack one's own trajectory is perfectly insidious. You often don't realize you're doing it.

To make any headway in the ninth house, we'll have to focus on what it is you want to do and what makes you happy, and then leave the analytics to Saturn. Old preconceptions won't get you very far, and inertia will not be an option; Saturn will likely force you into encounters with the teachers, guides, or mentors meant to usher you on your way. So you must signal that you're open and free of assumptions.

You'll notice that anyone who's been in a certain scene for too long—academia, soap opera writing, commercial piloting—tends to talk about the monoliths of their chosen field, the gatekeepers and ladders to climb, as if these things are real and unimpeachable, as if everyone knows about the rigorous admissions process to get into clown college. It's not to say that it's all in your head—that to succeed in any field, you don't have to pay your dues and endure certain rites—but Saturn will shake down any of the false ladders we've put too much faith in.

Of course, you could be a smashing success if it weren't for a certain someone, that gatekeeper, standing in your way. What is it about them? You can't put your finger on it, but they remind you of someone from your past, someone who often reinforced that your goals are unviable, that there is no free lunch, that you're better off not trying. It behooves me to keep bringing up dear old *Mutti* and *Vati* as Saturn's primary messengers, because it's likely that some projection of them is really holding you back, keeping you in your stagnant job, your lame old life. When Saturn returns to the ninth house, you'll have to confront the internalized messaging that keeps you from taking the leap. Nobody, no executive or pageant judge or Fortune 500 executive, is as frightening as your mother. Get clear on who is standing in for her, and you'll fear nothing.

Speaking of imposing gatekeepers, I should mention that the ninth house is the house of God. Consider who or what you've set up to be your god: how you've misplaced power, how you've ascribed total authority to false masters, and how you've already charted your trajectory without even taking off. Nearly every religion and sobriety program calls for surrender—or submission—to the will of a higher power, one who likely has a better plan in store for you than you do. It's not for me to force a faith on you, but it's worth investigating which false gods you're already worshipping or how you've set yourself up as queen of the universe, to be blamed for every single flaw in the plan.

Is there a spiritual practice, or even a mode of relational accountability, that releases you from the burden of omniscience? It's not easy to relinquish certainty over the future—but it's a relief, especially when you have a way of anticipating a negative outcome. Over this transit, it would help to find a regular practice, one that will allow you to release expectations so that Saturn can do its job.

I wish I could say that these rules only apply to sensitive twenty-seven-year-olds out to teach the world a lesson, but unfortunately, as we age, we tend to stagnate in limiting assumptions, and our view of the world around us, if not properly cultivated, has a way of shrinking. We think of the ninth house as the house of travel because there's nothing like seeing a new land to remind you of how small you are, how vast the world is, how endless the possibilities are. As you head toward your second Saturn Return, you may believe that you've seen it all, that you know it all, and that all that's left is a low hum of dread and boredom. This second Saturn Return in your ninth house will kick you out of the house. I should hope that you're in for a dazzling voyage to a far-off locale. But it may just be that you realize that you don't really believe in your politics anymore and that your friends have all become cranky old people. Go take some local classes, or attend lectures by radical thinkers. Find something thrilling. One way or another, you will be shaken out of complacency and returned to curiosity and excitement. It would be best if you didn't make this a struggle.

We all say that we want expansion, to live a life unbound by work and expectations, but few of us are brave enough to make the crossing: to embrace an open mind, to ride what comes and not set expectations, to confront complacency and force new habits. It's upsetting to realize how small we've kept it, how we've held ourselves back, and what's been lost to our blind spots along the way. And yet, when Saturn returns to the ninth house, it's not too late. Pack your bags. We're just getting started.

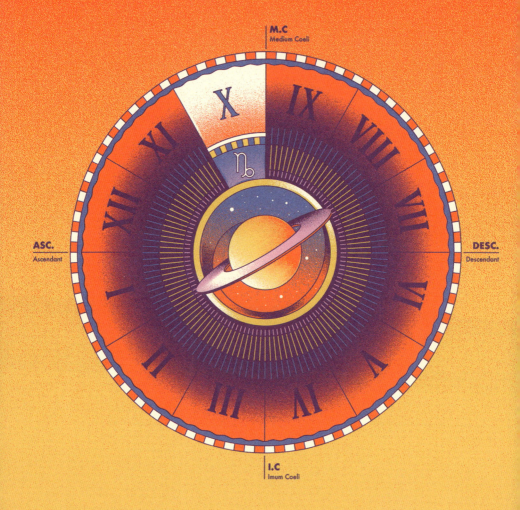

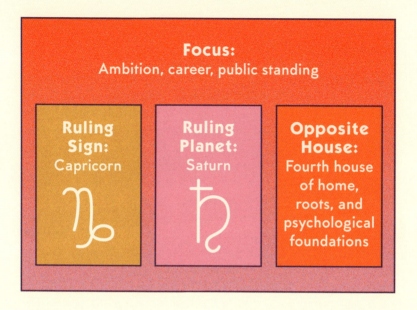

The long saga has brought us to something of a payoff point as Saturn returns to its home domain: the tenth house of ambition and public glory. This is where long-term plans bear fruit, where we may finally take repose in the splendor of our authority.

Of course . . . *ahem* . . . it doesn't always go quite according to plan. The stakes of the tenth house couldn't be higher; they represent the achievement of our capital *C* career goals, and here we run into a litany of risks, including but not limited to: depending too much on public acclaim to overcompensate for a lack of inner confidence, reaching for success to spite our parents, putting all our eggs in one basket.

Naturally, Saturn's endgame for you is to reach your most elevated potential, to slam it on the main stage, and to claim your role as a star in a bigger galaxy. But if this trajectory has corruptions in the design, they'll have to be faced head-on, ideally while you're still small-timing it and not once you've already made it to the public eye. When Saturn returns to the tenth house, your story of success is in for a major rewrite.

Let's begin with the fourth house, which sits directly opposite the tenth in your chart and represents your home, roots, family, and foundations. The fourth house is ostensibly ruled by the moon, the nourishing mommy archetype, while the tenth belongs to Saturn, the stern and authoritative father who brings home the bacon. We'll forgo any reductive gender ascriptions and get to it: Saturn's presence on this axis indicates the strong legacy of a parent figure, one who set before us vast and perhaps impossible expectations that we seek to fulfill in our public life. The fourth house provides us with information about *how* you were fed and if your parents gave you a sense of unconditional love and belonging.

As we arrive at the tenth house, we see how those gaps in our upbringing have grown and possibly metastasized. The legendary Molly Shannon has spoken about losing her mother when she was very young, and how, while on *Saturday Night Live*, she'd often look out at the audience, disappointed that it was missing the one person whose approval she craved. You may be on the biggest stage in the world, at the top of your game, but it's not enough to make you whole. When Saturn returns to the tenth house, you will have to return to your roots to consider what's been lost, and what no amount of money or achievement can make up for.

This process can be liberating, because if you can separate your present career from the expectations of your parents—or from your own drives to earn their love, spite them, or prove that they can't hurt you anymore—you're really free. Suddenly, what you do is just . . . what you do. It's not replacing anything, which means that the other areas of your life can flourish and the onus doesn't have to all be on your career.

When Saturn returns to the tenth house, it's highly likely that you'll experience some career flux, some lurch on the ladder to success. This can be shocking at first, but ideally, you should end this transit feeling more game to roll with the punches. Your industry may have rougher years, but you're OK, enjoying Jet Ski rides with your siblings, attending painting classes, watching Scandinavian murder mysteries. A crisis at the office, even if you happen to work in the Oval Office, doesn't spell out your immediate annihilation. There's more to you than this.

In this house, we consider the expectations laid out for us and the ladders we've elected to climb. This can lead to a sense of disillusionment. You may realize that it wasn't worth it, that, in fact, you don't want to be an orthodontist, and those grueling years in dental school were just to impress your father. Off to the youth hostel, where you'll work as a ski instructor until you find your real path.

That's one way it can go. Or things really *can* happen for you, all at once. I've had plenty of clients who have brought their career dreams to fruition and relished every moment of it. This is what they've been waiting for. But with exponentially more attention and responsibility, they have to learn to take care of themselves anew and firm up the balance with the fourth house, where they receive nourishment and support.

There are those whose tenth-house Saturn flattens them before they can launch. The success required to please your parents is so grand that you don't even bother getting started. As you near age thirty, you feel like a stagnant lump, terrified to try anything, buried by your fear of failure. There are also those who get so attached to one ambition, one role, that they won't consider anything else that Saturn sends their way.

The crises Saturn introduces in the tenth house are meant to break one's inertia and force them to consider their own versatility, and the possibility that they may be able to *do* more, *be* more, than what was laid out for them. Long before my Saturn

Return, I moved to Los Angeles to be a famous screenwriter. I met a lot of people who were similarly dogged; they came to the city to do one thing: act, write, sing, etc. Many of them would languish, waiting forever for that one vocation to take on. Years later, over my Saturn Return in New York, the city forced me to get flexible. It seemed like everyone did five things at once. If you wanted to be a comedian, you'd learn Photoshop so that you could market your shows . . . maybe there'd be some musical improv, so you should get ready with vocal warm-ups. It seemed like everyone was constantly discovering a new side of themselves.

Saturn's presence in the tenth house is meant to lead you to your highest potential, but for you to reap the benefits, you'll have to demonstrate that you're open to serving in a different role than previously expected; that you might be an actor who also directs and occasionally picks up bartending shifts, and that looks like a life you're happy to lead. The more desperately you cleave to some fixed plot, the more destruction Saturn will have to wreak in order to shake you loose.

As we approach your second and third Saturn Return, it's likely that you will indeed have taken on the role of master Saturn. So what is it all for? What is the point? Is this about your claiming power, hanging on to the CEO position for the sake of it, or is there some greater ethos spurring all this on? By now, questions of workaholism affecting your health will have been raised and possibly ignored. You'll have to really consider what winding down looks like and how you want to play the role of teacher to the next generation. The climb is over. Now we begin to look down and help others up.

It's impossible to purify one's ambitions under capitalism. That's fine. Saturn doesn't want you to rescind power, but to own it and channel it with intention. A tenth-house Saturn Return represents an arrival. The stakes are high, and more eyes are on you than ever before. The challenges of this house will purify your ambitions so that you can emerge as a leader and not a tyrant. It may seem selfish, to put so much into your own success, but if you wield the power responsibly, you can help others along their own paths. To do that, you'll have to take yourself, or your idea of yourself, out of the equation. Your destiny is meant to take you far. Get out of the way already.

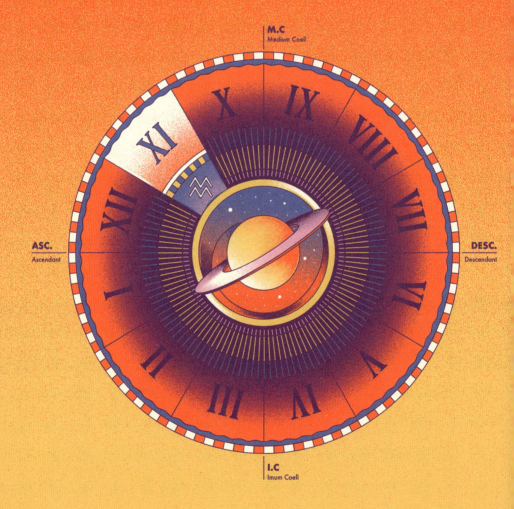

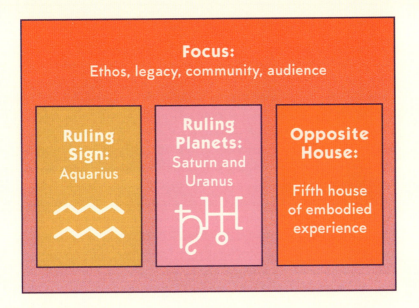

We've scaled the summit of your chart. You've won your Oscar, scored tenure, inherited the farm. Saturn will permit you to enjoy your achievements, and then, of course, it's back to the existential interrogation. It's time to ask what you're doing all this for, whom your work serves, and what it all means in the big picture. When Saturn returns to the eleventh house, you'll realize the mark you want to leave on the world.

I label the penultimate house of your chart as the domain of audience and legacy. We're facing questions of ethos, about where you fit into a larger constellation, what values make you an essential tile in the mosaic. Saturn speaks in the language of consequences, indicating to us (often harshly) the effects our actions have on ourselves and on others. In the eleventh house, we begin to comprehend the positive ways our impact can reverberate.

When we explored the fifth house of embodied expression, we came to understand what it is you *do*: the pleasure or passion that is yours to claim. Directly across the way, the eleventh house asks, *Once you've realized your talents, where do these gifts go?* If you had an audience, who would they be and what would they get out of your work? Here, we question the *why* behind your missions and inspirations.

To be clear, not everything in life has to be driven by some altruistic purpose or guiding star. There are some things we do because we just like doing them. But that doesn't mean they don't have an impact, especially on those around you. Let's say your passion is meeting up with the guys of your bowling league once a week. It may feel casual, but it's possible that you're influencing the lives of your teammates on deeper levels than you're aware of. Just the same, there's no measuring how they alter the course of your week or pull you out of your own myopia.

The things that matter to you likely do have some meaning to them. Maybe your love of baking connects you to your grandmother, and you want to carry on the feeling of being with her in the kitchen. Or, when you put your knack for numbers to use, helping your clueless clients file their taxes, you feel happy seeing their relief. Just identifying these seeds, these nuggets, can direct you toward meaning and how you want to follow it.

Saturn doesn't expect you to necessarily predict the measure of your gravitas, of how you and your work will change the world for better or worse. Questions of ethos and legacy have to be answered in dialogue with others. The assignment of the eleventh house is to find the people who align with your principles so that what you do serves them and the values that bind you together. This puts what you do, or what you enjoy, in perspective and conversation.

This is a pain in the ass, but we're really dealing with the matter of belonging. If you feel that you haven't found your people yet, Saturn will ask hard questions about how you're presenting yourself and if it authentically represents what you have to offer.

I've worked with many clients who have felt like they've arrived at their destined career but that they haven't found their peers yet. Often, they've handed false authority to perceived insiders, not realizing their own capacity to lead. Sometimes I send them on a journey to build their own *mishpucha*, but often it's about confronting those middle-school ideas we have of ourselves—they'll never accept me, I'm not good enough for them, I'm an alien. Inevitably, there is an ecosystem that not only has a place for you but also cannot grow or thrive without you. When Saturn returns to the eleventh house, you'll have to break down your outsider identity and take responsibility for the ways you've projected a false narrative of rejection and social exile.

A Saturn Return in any house will call for a severe audit of one's social life, but this time, we're evaluating the principles that connect you to others. When Saturn hit your seventh house, you were advised to break up with that toxic friend from your sorority years. In the eleventh house, you are questioning why you were in a sorority in the first place. Saturn wants to place you in your rightful community, which could refer to your local temple or even a global political network. These relationships have in common some shared passion, or point of view. You will more easily come to your purpose when you're actively inspired by the people around you.

When Saturn returns to the eleventh house, you will have to take risks to find your cohort. You'll learn how to show up solo to the local open-mic night or the dungeon rave. Saturn will indeed deliver you to your people, but only if you signal that you're serious about finding them. This will involve going your own way and establishing necessary space around friend groups that hold you back from discovering something new.

Just as often, you won't have to go far. Labor unions embody eleventh-house drives, recruiting fellow workers to show up for one another and ensure that power and protection is secure for all. Churches, synagogues, mosques, and community centers create avenues for support and celebration. Here, you're part of a larger whole.

So what is it that you're supposed to build? What does an eleventh-house Saturn want from you in the endgame? I often refer to this as the Dollywood placement, as Dolly Parton was born with Saturn in the eleventh. Naturally, Parton's career is an endless study in confidence, resurrection, and good business strategy. For me, the presence of Saturn in Parton's eleventh house leads us to the holy land of Dolly's divine legacy: her amusement park, not only a hub of communion for her fans but also an employment center for the inhabitants of her native land. Dollywood represents something beyond its titular empress because it brings her people—who happen to come from all manner of backgrounds—together. Even if it outlives Dolly, its service to her spiritual family endures.

In the eleventh house, your second and third Saturn Returns bring you toward your own Dollywood. You may realize that the ethics or principles that got you far are now considered narrow. Global conversations around political and social belonging move you to make your domain more supportive and inclusive. You revamp the institution you command—be it a capitalist enterprise or Bible study group—so that it can meet the needs of this era and serve the iteration to come. The eleventh house is a great village, and you are readying yourself to take on the role of leader and eventually elder. To do that, you cannot be rallying against the changing times.

I should mention, before it's too late, that the eleventh house is traditionally known as the house of hopes and wishes. Along with the tenth house, Saturn is exalted in the eleventh, and, at this point near the end of the saga, its return here represents years of work brought to a culmination. Sometimes one needs to pay an astrologer to remind them: You are entitled to achieve your goals, to bring your dreams to fruition, and to enjoy the spoils of your seeking. Face this Saturn Return, and the celebration won't be hollow. You'll be surrounded by the friends (and, perhaps, fans) with whom you are in challenging, inspiring dialogue. You'll feel committed to something bigger than your own success. In fact, all questions of *you* will begin to feel irrelevant as your gifts take root in something far greater. If ever there were a time to think big, it's now.

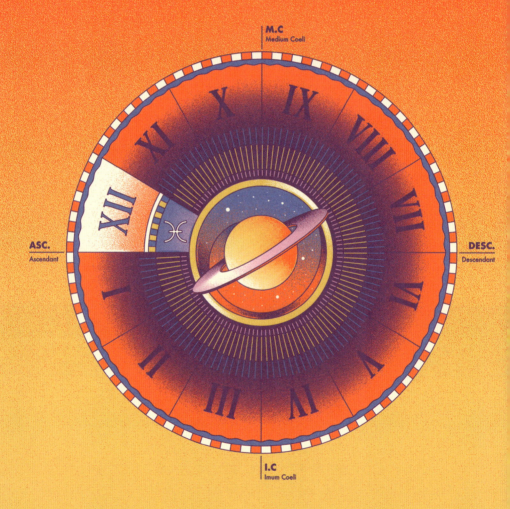

Twelfth House

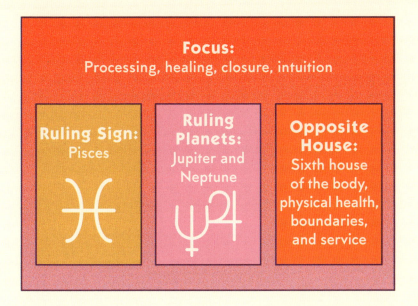

Saturn's arrival at the twelfth and final house marks the end of a very long journey, as it readies to end one revolution and begin another. Here, we have a rare chance at closure. When Saturn returns to the twelfth house, we heal the past so that a new cycle can begin.

If the chart launches at dawn, then the twelfth house represents a descent into the dark of night, a last voyage through the shadows before we emerge in the light of day. This is the repository of all that has been experienced in the preceding eleven houses, a spiritual antechamber that grinds down our history into fertilizer for the new consciousness already on its way. When the chart relaunches with the first house, so will our sense of awareness and identity. For now, we are in a nether-realm, beyond conscious awakening. When Saturn returns to the twelfth house, we must face what we've done and who we've been, and seek to light our way through the dark.

Forgive me if I sound like Cate Blanchett opening *The Lord of the Rings*, but the twelfth house is, by nature, a trippy domain. We're talking about the subconscious, the intuitive, numinous, and spiritual. Much of what's down here isn't visible—especially to you. This is where we contend with the behaviors that seem to erupt from within, no matter how they conflict with your external presentation. And it's where we find the drives that go beyond your waking programming. They need to be felt. They can't be put into words right away.

Astrologers have labeled the twelfth house as the asylum, hospital, therapist's couch, photographer's darkroom, or recording studio. It also constitutes a personal underworld, where buried treasure, ancient secrets, and what astrologer Robert Hand refers to as the "atomic arsenal" await those who know how to carefully spelunk.

Saturn is a planet of self-awareness. It's often Saturn's thankless job to reveal our blind spots, those vast and devastating valleys between our projected image and our behaviors. In twelve-step recovery programs, we learn to address our insobrieties and insanities, to quit pretending like we have a grip on forces beyond our control. When you admit that you really *do* become a different person while drinking and that you alone can no longer manage your addiction, you begin to take responsibility for your blind spots. This will, inevitably, ensure you make it through Saturn's next thirty-year tour of your chart, or that at least you won't actively sabotage it.

I bring up twelve-step programs because, as with most religions, they require a sacrifice of selfhood, a turning-over of the illusion of control. You will be led, here. That's not to say that a twelfth-house Saturn Return necessitates a rock-bottom moment out of *Euphoria*; rather, at this point in your life, you are ready to recognize how you've gotten in your way and what must change.

Twelve-step programs bring us into contact with our higher power, a force beyond us to which we can turn over our will and our lives. Saturn represents a higher authority, and its tenure in such a contemplative house often leads to spiritual breakthroughs and the embrace of religion. This is not about instant salvation or giving it all up to your cult leader. Saturn's too tough to fall for a fraud. Instead, the planet of structure will help you find a devotional practice or study that will give you guidance and accountability. You'll learn how to explore the numinous without losing your grip on reality.

The twelfth house is something of a greatest-hits montage of all the houses that have come before, leading you to reckon with family, upbringing, relationships, failures, and victories. Much is released here so that you can enter the rebirth of your chart with as little baggage as possible. I always advise clients undergoing a twelfth-house Saturn transit to give themselves this time to incubate in the dark. It's not that you have to become a witch in the woods, dead to society, but that you're best served wrapping up projects so that you can embrace a true new beginning soon, *when you're ready*.

Healing can yield surprising results. Saturn's presence in the twelfth house always points to gifts you didn't know you had, which can only be revealed in silence and solitude. Intuitive and creative faculties, talents and desires, sensations and feelings: The rewards will be vast, if you have the patience to dig past the external gunk that's calcified around your soul. By this point, you may have walked away from what was once life as you knew it. So you're not a Wall Street beast anymore, doing eight balls every night after fifteen-hour workdays. But lo, after moving back in with your parents and attending NA meetings, you start to tap into a well of sensitivities you'd buried long ago. Maybe you're an artist, a healer, a channel, or one of those people who sell homemade focaccia at 6:00 a.m. at the farmers market. I don't know. But Saturn's brought you this far. You'll have to trust that there's a plan underway here.

You will not only heal yourself through this house. The twelfth arms you with the perspective to empathize with anyone, to step in and spare others from the pain you've experienced. As Korra reflects on *The Legend of Korra*: "I needed to understand what true suffering was, so that I could be more compassionate to others."

We've talked self-sabotage. But one should also beware of self-sacrifice. If you've lived a life of martyrdom, stuck in a caretaker position for a loved one, you'll be forced to break the codependent streak here. We're too close to the jubilant independence of the first house—you can no longer live for others. Your own repressed desires and rage will come to combustion here. If you've feared taking up space, now's when you face the monster within and embrace its power.

We've hopefully established, by this point, that in astrology, all opposites are two sides of a coin. We studied the sixth house, the domain of the body and its healthy functioning. The twelfth, across the way, is the shadow realm of the mind. It's rare for a client to bring up a medical crisis without there being some deeper resonance. Unprocessed grief, repressed memories, stifled rage, familial violations: These have a way of registering somatically. When Saturn returns to the twelfth house, you'll have to heal these wounds holistically and, in so doing, gain access to body, mind, and spirit. This ensures a healthier, more balanced life cycle to come.

Naturally, in your midfifties and eighties, you should have plenty to reflect upon. That's not to say that you're consigned to an unending shiva by your second or third Saturn Return, or that you're cursed to live in the past. Rather, you're invited to close out one era so that you may walk eagerly into the next. If Saturn has you cleaning out the basement, arranging your photo albums, or writing your memoirs, it means that you're meant to look back now so that you may soon look forward. Take this time, and be excited that you may be around for another revolution.

Interacting with twentysomethings always proves fascinating. Some are still the protagonists of their own stories, still in the eye of the hurricane. And then there are the ones who have crossed through, let something go, come out of the underworld whole.

Those with a Saturn Return in their twelfth house will emerge as vessels of perspective. They'll have put the past behind them so that they can be present for what lies ahead. They'll teach the rest of us the way. If this is your karmic assignment, we need you to hang in there so that you can teach the rest of us how it's done.

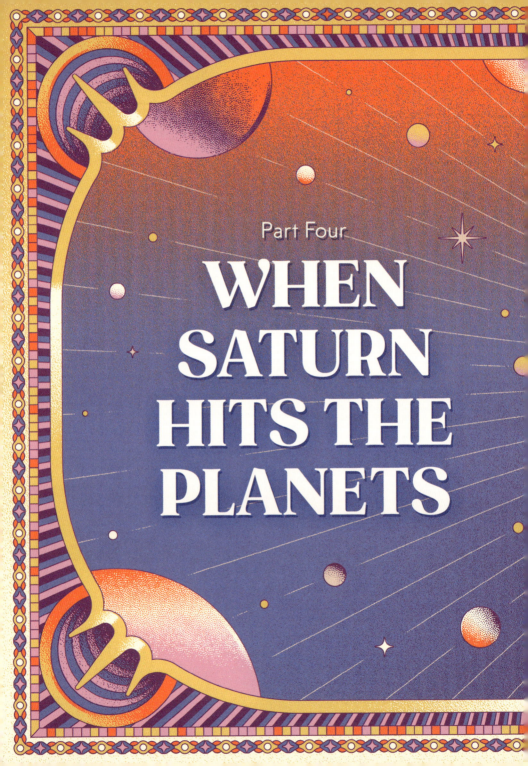

SATURN AND THE PERSONAL PLANETS

A dear client of mine, upon turning thirty-two, let me have it: Her Saturn Return was long over . . . and yet, she still felt like a Victorian poetess dying of consumption, a martyr on the altar. "When is it going to get easier?" she asked desperately. Indeed, her chart revealed that Saturn was not *yet* done with her, as it was opposing her sun, Mars, and Venus in rapid succession. She had a bit more cooking to do.

The personal planets—the sun, moon, Mercury, Venus, Mars, and to some extent Jupiter—are indeed personal. Their arrangement in your chart is specific to you. As Saturn continues its endless march through your chart, it will inevitably interact with these primary players, setting off cataclysms meant to inspire sharper redefinition. We look at the placement of your birth planets to understand the fundamentals of who you are. As Saturn hits them, they are challenged and refined. The form and context of these events will be determined by the planet in question, the houses involved, and the signs at play.

Before we get into the nature of these planetary convergences, let's review the menu. Remember that Saturn takes about twenty-eight years to complete a revolution, so you can expect some angle (0 degrees, 90 degrees, 120 degrees, 180 degrees) to every planet, just about every seven years. You want to know the exact degree of the planet involved (there are 30 degrees in every sign and house). Saturn spends about eight days per degree, but considering that it retrogrades—moves forward, backward, and forward again—it may well put a particular planet through multiple rounds rather than just one.

And the effects may be felt for some time, before and after Saturn interacts directly with a planet. If, say, you're a Scorpio, you should be aware of Saturn's coming Taurus tour (2028–2030). Though Saturn may only directly oppose your sun for a few days, it's still staring it down from the opposite side of the chart. With that in mind, you won't see the coming challenges as shocks or ambushes.

Here are all the different forms of planetary interactions:

- **Conjunction:** When a transiting planet comes into alignment with the natal position of another planet. Let's say you were born with your sun at a certain degree of Gemini. As Saturn approaches that exact position, it becomes conjunct with your natal sun, forcing a total reappraisal of your external identity. If you're an Aries, Saturn's 2025–2028 tour will force you to declare your independence under fire.

- **Trine:** At 120 degrees apart, two planets form a supportive aspect to one another. They will be in two signs of the same element. Perhaps you were born with your moon in Libra. As Saturn comes into Gemini, it forms a helpful trine to your moon, helping you set boundaries for your social reality.

- **Square:** At a perpendicular aspect of 90 degrees apart, two planets come to challenge one another. I call this a "backseat driver" position, as Saturn will, in my mother's words, *noodge* another planet, questioning its drives and throwing wrenches in its plans. Say you were born with Mars in the dreamworld of Pisces. When Saturn hits Virgo, 90 degrees apart, it squares your Mars, forcing it to get organized and make a plan.

- **Oppositions:** When two planets face each other directly across the chart, they are in an opposition. At 180 degrees apart, this is a classic showdown, not meant to initiate a deadlock but to inspire growth, learning, and perspective. If Saturn opposes one of your natal planets, it is like a comic book supervillain forcing the hero to stand up and prove themselves under adversity.

Saturn and the sun

Consider our heroine before she enters the training montage: Goldie Hawn in *Private Benjamin*, Fa Mulan, Uma Thurman in *Kill Bill: Volume 2*. We see the potential, the glimmer of radiance, but it is not until she has met her stern master and contemplated the face of her nemesis that she comes into warriorhood. The sun is your identity and individuality, which must occasionally be put through the ringer to emerge defined. Saturn will act as a hard teacher, making it harder for your sun to rise. These transits often feel like a shutdown of your established identity, a drain to one's vitality. Saturn intends not to eliminate you but to strip away the dead skin and expired attributes of self. Whoever comes out of the mud is leaner and more confident in their intrinsic identity, no longer dependent on the old signifiers they were relying upon. You will recover from this, stronger than ever. But you'll have to let yourself take a few hits along the way. As with a Saturn Return period, you should consider the entirety of Saturn's tour through your sun sign as a period of growth by trial. The substance and nature of the lessons will be cohesive throughout.

Saturn and the moon

    This is about as climactic a showdown of opposites as you can get. Saturn, as established, represents a hard-ass daddy, firmly shaking your hand at Thanksgiving and asking how you're going to make a living. The moon, meanwhile, is the mother avatar, our tidal source of love and emotion. I think of a Saturn-moon transit as a point of resolution, when, back against the wall, you are forced to defend your emotional needs at all costs. You can no longer compromise on them. Saturn will question the ways you deal with and feed yourself: Is this nourishment, or dissociation? By shedding outdated coping mechanisms and affirming the value of your sensitivities, you emerge knowing how to better take care of yourself and receive love from others.

Saturn and Mercury

Mercury is the messenger, or "doer," of the gods, and so represents your personal field of finite action. Through Mercury, we see how you organize your thoughts and daily facilities, your interactions, the way everything functions. Saturn arrives as a haughty business consultant, reviewing all the inefficiencies that have kept you from achieving your full potential. You may feel everything grind to a halt during these transits, but their ultimate purpose is to bring order to the ways you structure your mind. Consider new modes of self-expression and more integrated ways of functioning on a daily basis. This is meant to be productive . . . and even fun.

Saturn and Venus

In this configuration, Saturn is less of a boot camp instructor and more of a makeover coach, à la Michael Caine in *Miss Congeniality* or Julie Andrews in *The Princess Diaries*. Taste, creativity, and self-presentation are honed here, not only to help you land a date but also to master your artistic potential. Saturn will force your Venus to define herself: What brings you delight? How can you afford it? Who, or what, is obstructing it? The reward for enduring these periods of deprivation is the elevation of authentic creative experience. Venus wants you to more presently experience the world. Saturn will make the romantic real.

Saturn and Mars

What is the point of your ambition? Whom does your rebellion serve? Where will your desires lead you? It's always a bummer for our inner warrior to be audited, but Saturn, as the stern father, must occasionally put his teenage son through the ringer. When properly channeled, Mars delivers us to power and prominence: You are an active, integrated body fulfilling a purpose. But often our wires get crossed, our release valves stuck, our motivations scrambled. Saturn will force you to align your drives to a higher purpose, sometimes by confronting misdirected rage, adolescent petulance, and your complicated relationship with authority. On the other side of this transit is an end to the tantrum and the embrace of your own true authority.

♃
Saturn and Jupiter

 Until just a few centuries ago, Jupiter and Saturn were thought to be the final planets in our solar system. Jupiter, a glorious gas giant, collects the wisdom and power of the preceding planets into synthesis. This is your best self, ready to hurl lightning and take the throne on Mount Olympus. Saturn's wish for Jupiter is to set our dreams, goals, and flashes of glory in stone, to make something real out of the drug-trip realizations. Saturn's dialogue with Jupiter may feel like a bummer, but its purpose is, as always, constructive: What modes of accountability are required to make something out of all this potential? Another confrontation with a gatekeeper, solidifying the strength and firmament of your dreams.

SATURN AND THE GENERATIONAL PLANETS

Moving past Saturn, we encounter the dark masters: Uranus, Neptune, and Pluto. Because these planets take years to cross through a single sign, and many decades to complete a revolution through the zodiac, their impact is felt collectively rather than personally. You likely share these planetary placements with everyone in your generation.

Saturn's interaction with these planets, in their natal positions in your chart, will take on an immediately karmic verve. There is a sense of a larger gate being crossed, of making it through a door to destiny. Saturn is trying to situate you within a larger human narrative, which means that the rearrangements tend to be more dramatic. With the personal planets, you may feel as though something's off or you're going through a hard week. Often, the involvement of the generational planets will feel like a thumb from heaven is nudging you around, like you're a piece on a board. Again, as always, you are not being targeted but rather repositioned to be of the highest good to everyone involved.

Saturn and Uranus

Like the lightning harnessed by Dr. Frankenstein to reanimate his monster, the crackling electricity of Uranus awakens. This is a rebellious current, which brings one into larger movements, politics, and schools of thought. Over the years, many of us calcify into complacency or stagnation, living the lives our parents laid out for us. As Saturn and Uranus interact, they guide us through our own chaotic revivals. I often tell clients that the big bad wolf has come to blow the house down. But behold: With the roof off and the windows shattered, you have a clear view of the world around you. You can leave the ranch now. Saturn has every intention of shepherding you out of your myopic little cul-de-sac as Uranus blasts your mind open. It's important to find accountable means of reflection and study so that you don't get lost in performative radicalism. We are trying to inspire genuine, life-changing thought here. This transit is meant to bring you closer to reality, not into conspiracy thinking and misguided rebellion.

Saturn and Neptune

Neptune is our link to the rainbow bridge, to the full spectrum of shared human empathy and imagination. Neptune's presence in one's chart points to the doors of spiritual vessel-hood, and, through the same door, to those addictions or delusions that will lead to one's undoing. This is a powerful current to channel, and with Saturn's help, one can build the submarine required to safely pass. Saturn has not come to crush your sensitivity or romantic nature, but to bring them into healthy, stable function. These transits help you channel creativity and inspiration without losing yourself along the way.

Saturn and Pluto

Pluto is the planet of karma, the god of death. When Orpheus rescued his beloved Eurydice from the underworld, he was instructed to not look back—or else. Indeed, when Saturn's drive to restructure your life leads you down into your personal underworld, you will have to put something—a lifestyle, an identity, a sense of social belonging—to rest once and for all. There is a Pyrrhic sense of closure here, which allows you to fully move forward. This is why when we visit places where we once lived and see the people who were once everything to us, we realize that we can't go back. What's done is done, and only by surrendering to Saturn and Pluto's plan for us can we ensure that the past won't repeat. Let it burn.

CONCLUSION

Saturn Incarnate

By the side of the everlasting Why there is a Yes—a transitory Yes, if you like, but a Yes.
—E. M. Forster, A Room with a View

People used to instruct me, in my twenties, to enjoy these salad days. "You're so young!" they'd exclaim. I wanted to tell them how old I felt, like a broken-down jalopy, how every moment dragged on under the agony of my own dissociative and shaming tendencies. I already felt dead much of the time.

And so Saturn came to finish the job. Nearly every aspect of "me" was tossed into the incinerator. It was the end of life as I knew it. And yet, I came to realize that Saturn had given me a choice. If I was willing to commit, I could start anew, on my terms. Dreams would have to be ditched, losses absorbed, pain felt. I signed my name and showed up. The clock restarted, and someone began to take shape in the blur of the Polaroid.

I feel younger now, in my midthirties, than I ever did, even when I was a teenager. There are moments of delight and discovery, sometimes just while I'm washing dishes. And they feel well-earned. I choose to be here, which means I get to enjoy it.

I wish I could tell you that at the end of your first Saturn Return, you'll be able to kick back and enjoy the spoils of battle, sleeping off those first thirty years under a thatched tiki roof. By this point you understand the ambivalences inherent in astrology's cyclical nature: The wheel will keep on spinning. There are no endings.

And yet, in my friends and clients, I have witnessed the spectacular. People get better, they recover. They come into themselves and find each other. When it comes to Saturn, there is such a thing as closure.

After your Saturn Return is over, it's inevitable that Uranus and Pluto will have something planned for you, or that Saturn's next angle will put you through it all over again, like you're the final girl in a slasher-movie sequel. Still, with each passing revolution, you see yourself less as a victim and more as a passenger. As Saturn knocks you off your ass, you roll your eyes, this time allowing it to offer you a hand back up. You move through the trials, then get back to the life you've created for yourself: the relationships you've cultivated, the family you've built, the dreams you've made real, the values you honor. Or maybe you just have to walk the dog and can't spend too much time rehashing grievances.

Nothing ever ends, and with every one of Saturn's turnings, we return to those blind spots and bad behaviors that prove our self-undoing. Saturn cannot destroy that which is built to endure. Whatever, or whoever, survived the last trial with us remains. This time and the next, we return with more patience, more humor, more of ourselves, just more. Inevitably, that will be enough to make us realize that it's all been worth it, and that we have so much yet to look forward to.

GLOSSARY

Angle: A dialogue between planets based on geometric configurations, i.e., a 90-degree square, 180-degree opposition, etc. Angles put planets into conflict or collaboration, setting off an archetypal conversation.

Ascendant: The sign, at its exact degree, rising over the eastern horizon at the time of your birth. This marks the beginning and end of your chart and will also play the all-important role of your "rising sign." The ascendant sets the genre and direction of your chart and cannot be calculated without knowing one's exact birth time.

Aspect: Any contact between planets. Two planets come into aspect whether by conjunction, opposition, sextile, square, or trine. The nature of the planets involved and the angle of interaction will inform us of the archetypal meaning at stake.

Cardinal sign: The first sign of each of the four seasons: Aries launches the spring, Cancer the summer, Libra the fall, and Capricorn the winter. Defined by a spirit of initiatory, active propulsion.

Conjunction: An aspect in which two planets are within 5 degrees of each other. This can play out as an archetypal sharing of resources or a competition for space. One may have planets conjunct in their birth chart, or track the conjunction of transiting planets with their natal planets. For example, if transiting Saturn crosses over the position of your natal sun, you are experiencing a Saturn-sun conjunction.

Degrees: Every sign and every house has 30 degrees, which function as units of time in the tracking of planetary movement. Consider these seconds on a clock, exact markers of a planet's location at any given time. Saturn moves about 12 degrees a year. Based on its degree, we can identify which other planets it is interacting with and in what time frame. Using an ephemeris, or calendar of planetary correspondences, we can determine a planet's degree down to the hour.

Descendant: Dusk in your chart. Located at the eastern edge, at the start of your seventh house of others. The descendant is a convergence point for relationships and launching one's "debut" into public visibility.

Glossary

Detriment: Every planet has a ruling, or home, sign. When it is in the opposite sign, it is in its detriment, where it is thought to struggle. Saturn rules global-minded Aquarius, meaning that it is in its detriment in self-centered Leo.

Elements: The four signs are broken into four elements: fire (Aries, Leo, Sagittarius); earth (Taurus, Virgo, Capricorn); air (Gemini, Libra, Aquarius); water (Cancer, Scorpio, Pisces). Commonly, earth and water are considered to be a harmonious pairing, and air works well with fire. Regardless, any chart will have some variety of planets in different elements, which allows for a rich interpretation of how they express themselves.

Ephemeris: A calendar of astrological correspondences, listing which degree every planet will hit on any given day of any month or year. You can find free ephemerides online or purchase them in print.

Exaltation: Every planet has a sign of rulership, or its home domain, and a sign of exaltation, where it gets along well. Saturn is exalted in Libra, the sign of social harmony.

Fall: Opposing the sign of a planet's exaltation is where it is fallen. Saturn thrives in directorial Libra but is in its fall in single-minded Aries.

Fixed sign: The middle sign of the season: Taurus at the heart of the spring, Leo in the peak heat of summer, Scorpio in the autumn, and Aquarius at winter's darkest. These signs embody and articulate the themes of the season.

Generational planets: Saturn, Uranus, Neptune, and Pluto. Because these planets are farther from the sun, their orbit is slower. Spending years in a sign (as opposed to the personal planets, which occupy a sign for a few weeks), their influence is felt collectively.

Houses: The twelve lenses through which we view the birth chart and understand one's place in their journey. Each house has a specific meaning or assignment, and the layout of the signs and planets over the houses is determined by the placement of the ascendant or rising sign, which begins the chart.

Imum Coeli: Midnight in your chart. This line marks the base of your chart, around your fourth house of roots and family. It informs us of your core conditioning.

Midheaven: Known also as the MC, this line represents noon in your chart, and is located around your tenth house of career and public glory. This is a marker of visibility and the realization of ambition.

Mutable sign: Arriving at the end of a season and facilitating the transition into the next. Gemini wraps the spring, Virgo ends summer and prepares us for the fall, Sagittarius buttons up fall and readies us for the cold months with gusto, and Pisces closes out the winter for the awakening of spring. Their nature is reactive, liquid, and dialogic.

Natal: Refers to the positioning of the planets at the time of your birth. Their placement is specific to you. A Saturn Return refers to transiting Saturn's return to its natal position in your chart.

Opposition: An aspect in which two planets come into a 180-degree face-off. This may be a battle of primal forces, a deadlock, or, hopefully, a conflict meant to initiate growth and compromise. Oppositions may occur in one's natal chart, between currently transiting planets, or when a transiting planet comes into 180-degree alignment with a planet in the birth chart. An opposition will usually occur between signs of the same triplicity.

Personal planets: The sun, moon, Mercury, Venus, Mars, and, to some extent, Jupiter. These planets move through the signs at a fast clip, so their reverberations hit you in the immediate. Jupiter spends a year or so in each sign, so its effects can be thought of as both personal and generational.

Placement: The location of a planet, in a sign and house. You could refer to some placements as more difficult or advantageous than others.

Planets: The ten core archetypes of astrology, each with its own characteristics and drives. In their movement through the signs and interaction with one another, the planets push the story forward and inform us of what's going on in the moment. Each planet rules a sign, making it the emissary of the sign's ideas. As astrology is a geocentric study, the Earth does not count as a planetary archetype, while the sun, itself the center of our solar system, metaphorically "moves" through the signs. Everyone is born with all ten planets active in their chart, just as they are all active at present.

Retrogrades: When we, Earth-dwellers, "catch up" to another planet's orbit, it produces the illusory phenomenon of the other planet falling backward. Save for the sun and moon, all planets retrograde, many of them on an annual basis. As a planet moves forward, lurches back, and then resumes course, it inspires something of a review or necessary retracing of one's steps.

Rulership: A planet's home domain. Each sign is a collection of ideas, with its ruling planet acting as its emissary. Saturn rules Capricorn and co-rules Aquarius, with Uranus. Every sign has its own ruler or rulers.

Sextile: An aspect in which two planets at 60 degrees apart produce a sympathetic, supportive partnership. Sextiles may occur in one's natal chart, between transiting planets, or when a transiting planet comes into 60-degree alignment with a planet in the birth chart. These usually form within complementary signs, i.e., fire and air, or water and earth.

Square: An aspect in which two planets at 90 degrees apart enter a challenge. I call this the "backseat driver" aspect, as one forces the other to step up its game. Squares may occur in one's natal chart, between currently transiting planets, or when a transiting planet comes into 90-degree alignment with a planet in the birth chart. Squares will usually go down among signs of the same triplicity.

Transit: A planet's movement through a sign or house. When talking about transiting planets, we refer to their position in the cosmos at this moment, as opposed to one's natal planets, or those found in the birth chart.

Trine: An aspect in which two planets align at 120 degrees and become collaborators and mutual supporters. Trines usually go down within two signs of the same element. Trines may occur in one's natal chart, between currently transiting planets, or when a transiting planet comes into 120-degree alignment with a planet in the birth chart.

Triplicity: The seasonal breakdown of sign types: Cardinal signs launch the season, fixed signs embody its core tenets, and mutable signs close out its story. Signs within the same triplicity share similar drives and ways of functioning. When a planet interacts with another in the same triplicity, they will likely come into square or opposition.

ACKNOWLEDGMENTS

Years ago, sick in bed on my birthday, I received my first book of astrology, along with a bouquet of flowers, from Chani Nicholas and Sonya Passi. They knew I was curious, and that I just needed the right push. It was a copy of Richard Tarnas's *Cosmos and Psyche*, which I gulped down in a state of delirium. From then on, I was obsessed, reading every astrological text I could get my hands on. Soon after, Henry Koperski invited me to share thoughts on the movement of the planets at a "Teleological Meeting" he was hosting. I'd never done anything like that. Then Shayna Blass asked me to read her chart. I'd never done that either.

If you read this book, you know by now that nothing is incidental. These small gestures from loved ones were enough to set me on my path, inspiring me to pursue this seriously. I started my own business, reading charts and tarot cards for clients all over the world. Soon, my old friend Layla Halabian took a risk and recruited me to write *NYLON*'s astrology column, encouraging me to learn as I go. We had a blast together. My column would catch the attention of Emma Brodie at Chronicle Books, who was looking for someone to write about Saturn.

This book could not have come to term without Emma's vision and the patient direction of my editor, Maddy Wong, along with Cara Bedick. My brother, Danny, provided critical advice regarding the legalese and helped me feel less helpless at my most vulnerable. Jake Cornell, Tawny Lara, Harry James Hanson, and Amy Kiberd offered essential business insight.

Saturn often takes the form of harsh teachers, but by grace you're sometimes delivered a healer, a guide to help you through the underworld. I learned to listen, to channel, and to counsel from Mikella Millen, Kat Hunt, and Devin Antheus. These were the loving mentors of my Saturnian initiation.

Acknowledgments

I was largely broke while writing this text, and so it fell to Albina Shtutman to keep me fed and nourished along the way. I am whole, completing this book and looking forward to the next, because of her care. My aunt Yoda and friends Ryan Amador and Emily Dacey saw me through tricky patches. Lulu Krause and Emily Olcott always asked the right questions and never forced unwanted advice. There were times when I felt too weak to face Saturn in the arena, and Daniel Lax stood as my champion. I would have given up if he hadn't had my back.

My mother is a Taurus, like me, and from time immemorial has pointed out the legends who share our sign, on stage and screen. It became a source of pride. *They're our people.* I wonder if I'd see the cosmos through culture, or read ancient archetypes as alive and dazzling, without her influence. Her joy of expression is in the DNA of this book.

At my sixth-grade Halloween party, my stepmother pulled out a tarot deck and read our fortunes. She introduced me to *Buffy the Vampire Slayer* and to the possibility of worlds beyond suburbia. Thanks to her, my path would never be predictable.

Among all the masters I've encountered, none are wiser than my father. I've inherited many gifts from him, but of the most precious is his love of language. For me, writing has always been a joy, a place of delight, and that's because of him.

But the deepest gratitude is owed to my clients. It's said among astrologers that the reading you give is the one you're meant to receive. Over hundreds of hours, my clients have reflected optimism, creativity, and complexity to me, coaching me in humility as they've bared their pain. This book is an archive of just some of the lessons I've learned from them. It's an honor to have their trust, and yours, and to call this my job.

ABOUT THE AUTHOR

David Odyssey is a writer, astrologer, and magician. He is the former astrology columnist for *NYLON* and since 2019 has hosted *The David Odyssey Show*, a podcast covering cosmos and culture. He offers private astrological and tarot readings remotely and writes personal essays and reflections on his Substack.

Since 2007, David has covered LGBTQ art and culture, writing for *Vulture*, *GAWKER*, *Dazed*, *OutSmart*, *Entertainment Weekly*, and other publications. He is a former editor at *Time Out New York* and has performed original work on stages all over New York City.

David has worked with hundreds of clients, through all manner of metamorphoses, and has taught courses on astrology, tarot, and beyond. He is an initiate in the Dionysian Mysteries and a proud Jew.